He Must Be The One

A verse by verse study of Colossians

By Dr. Dino Pedrone

Xulon PRESS

Table of Contents

Dedication

Dedicated to Dr. and Mrs. Clyde Box. Clyde Box is a preacher of preachers. Few are able to proclaim the truth with the oratorical ability of Clyde Box. Dr. and Mrs. Box are the epitome of a happy and loving couple. I personally appreciate their input into my life.

Forward

Forty years is considered a generation. For forty years, I preached as a pastor. Hours were spent weekly in the confines of a study surrounded by several thousand books on shelves and huge amounts of literature available on my computer. Then, week after week with fear and trembling, I would stand before congregations to preach the amazing truths of the Bible. I am convinced that preaching is at the heart of ministry.

I am now past forty years in the ministry. Sunday after Sunday I stand before a congregation in a different town or city and preach. As the president of an amazing school, Davis College (a school dedicated to sending men and women into the ministry), it is my honor to represent our institution by sharing a few words about our college and then proclaiming the truths of God's Word.

This commentary you are reading is not an academic commentary. It is the third commentary (Ephesians and Romans previously) that is presented basically as it was given from the pulpit to congregations. This commentary is very practical and it is given in the spirit of preaching! As you read the commentary, it is best to have an open Bible and to visualize a church service with the preacher expounding God's Word.

It is a privilege, honor, and ultimate joy to proclaim God's truth. We need preaching today. We therefore need preachers. My advice to all preachers it to do just that. Preach expositionally and practically the eternal Word of God. There are numerous people who need to hear it!

Introduction

"There's no place like this place, anywhere near this place. So this must be the place!" These were the words on a sign of an obscure service station in a hill town of Kentucky. My good friend, Bible conference speaker, author, and pastor Tom Wallace said he found this sign at a service station as he and his wife traveled at dusk one night searching for gasoline for their automobile. A gas gauge on empty, few towns, and almost no connection with civilization at dusk by anxious vacationers made this small seemingly insignificant building with a gas pump (still pumping gas) a welcome sight.

The New Testament book of Colossians presents a truth that is central to the Christian faith. The Trinitarian conviction that God the Father, Son, and Spirit are one is clearly explained in this small, four chapter epistle. A quick perusal, however, declares that there is something special about God the Son. There is one God fully revealed in three persons. This epistle states there is a Savior sent from the Father who witnesses to us through the Holy Spirit. In taking a thought from the statement of our out-of-the-way service station sign, the book of Colossians declares, "There is no Savior, like this Savior, anywhere near this Savior. So He must be the one!" It is this author's prayer that the reader will focus as they study this commentary on the Lord Jesus Christ (He's the one!).

Chapter One

FOCUSING ON THE TRINITY

"Paul, an apostle of Jesus Christ by the will of God, and Timotheus our brother, to the saints and faithful brethren in Christ which are at Colosse: Grace be unto you, and peace, from God our Father and the Lord Jesus Christ. We give thanks to God and the Father of our Lord Jesus Christ, praying always for you, since we heard of your faith in Christ Jesus, and of the love which ye have to all the saints, for the hope which is laid up for you in heaven, whereof ye heard before in the word of the truth of the gospel; which is come unto you, as it is in all the world; and bringeth forth fruit, as it doth also in you, since the day ye heard of it, and knew the grace of God in truth: As ye also learned of Epaphras our dear fellowservant, who is for you a faithful minister of Christ; who also declared unto us your love in the Spirit." (**Colossians 1:1-8**)

A few years ago I was enjoying a visit from the former president of Luther Rice Seminary, Gene Williams, who encouraged me to enter a doctoral program through the seminary. I decided to do it. This was a program of three to eight years, during which I would go to the campus for a week at a time, return home with many books and other materials, write papers, go back to the campus, and continue the same process. I decided to complete the program in three years because that cost less money.

The first year was really exciting. I would get up at 4:30 a.m. and go into my study with a cup of coffee, still wearing my pajamas, to focus on the program for about two hours. There were books to read, tapes to listen to, and papers to write. When my alarm clock went off I would jump out of bed because I was excited about the program. This lasted for a few months.

About six months to a year after I started, that same alarm clock looked like a dragon to me. It went off in the wee hours of the morning. Sometimes I would push the snooze button and sleep for another 15 or even 30 minutes. In the second year I was behind in the program.

I remember telling my wife, "I'm going to kill it or it's going to kill me, but I want to get this done in three years so I don't have to spend any more money." I was able to finish, but it took a great deal of focus in the final months for me to accomplish it. Staying focused is hard. Notice in this section three things to focus on involving our wonderful God revealed in three persons, the Father, Son, and Holy Spirit.

We need to focus on our **faith**. In the opening verses of Colossians, Paul emphasizes that he is speaking as an ambassador of God by a divine appointment that has been given to him. Notice in verse 2 his reference to "*the saints and faithful brethren.*" The epistle is addressed to them. When we come to Christ and have Him in our lives we are considered saints of God. This phrase describes the divine relationship each of us has with God.

There are many ideas about how one becomes a Christian. Some believe, as one man told me a few weeks ago, "I have been a Christian all my life."

Another will say, "I am a Christian because I am a member of such-and-such church." Being a member of a certain church does not make you a Christian, nor does a lifetime of good deeds.

To focus on our faith we need to fully understand what exactly constitutes our faith. Let's look briefly at three biblical examples that illustrate what it means to be a Christian.

The first is in John 3, where we read about a prominent Pharisee named Nicodemus who wanted to meet with Jesus and came at night so his friends would not know about the meeting.

Nicodemus began with a compliment, saying to Jesus in verse 2, "*Rabbi, we know that thou art a teacher come from God: for no man can do these miracles that thou doest, except God be with him.*" The term "rabbi" was reserved for the most respected religious teachers of the day.

Jesus skipped over the nice words and went straight to the heart of the matter in verse 3. "*Jesus answered and said unto him, verily, verily, I say unto thee, except a man be born again, he cannot see the kingdom of God.*" Some people today tend to avoid using the phrase "born again" in favor of more modern terminology, but that is what Christ used and I would prefer to use it because it has great meaning.

In verse 4 Nicodemus asks the obvious question. "*Nicodemus saith unto him, how can a man be born when he is old? Can he enter the second time into his mother's womb, and be born?*"

That leads to a series of important statements by Jesus. One of them is in verse 6: "*That which is born of the flesh is flesh; and that which is born of the Spirit is spirit.*" Another is found in verse 8: "*The wind bloweth where it listeth, and thou hearest the sound thereof, but canst not tell whence it cometh, and whither it goeth: so is every one that is born of the Spirit.*"

Jesus then takes the discussion to one of the most famous verses in the Bible, verse 16: "*For God so loved the world, that he gave his only begotten Son, that whosoever believeth in him should not perish, but have everlasting life.*"

In that verse, He emphasizes to Nicodemus that God is the source of salvation, having loved mankind so much that He would make the ultimate sacrifice, and we can have eternal life through Him. That, as the late evangelist B.R. Lakin said, is "the Gospel in a nutshell."

Everyone is a sinner. It's not just that we commit sins, but it is the root problem. We are not sinners because we sin, but we sin because we are sinners. I cannot work my way into Heaven because when God looks at me He sees my sin. Not only am I lost, but I cannot do anything good enough to merit eternal life.

Church membership, baptism, putting money in the offering plate – are all good things, but none of that affects whether you are born again. We must realize that the Gospel is about Christ's death, burial and resurrection for us (I Corinthians 15:1-5), and we must receive Him into our lives as Savior, recognizing that we are lost without Him. He is the only One who can save us and cleanse our sins.

The next illustration is in John 4, where Jesus is traveling through Samaria on His way to Galilee. The Samaritans were considered half-breeds. Both Jews and Gentiles abhorred them. When Jesus came to the well and asked the Samaritan woman for a drink of water, she was surprised that He even spoke to her because He was a Jew and she was a Samaritan, and also because she was a woman and He was a man.

When He told her that He could give her living water, she did not really comprehend what He was saying. He showed her that she was a sinner by telling her to call her husband and then revealing that she had not only had five previous husbands but was at that time living with a man to whom she was not married.

"How do you know all of this?" she asked. She soon learned who Jesus was, and she went back to her town saying, *"Come, see a man, which told me all things that ever I did: is not this the Christ?"* (verse 29) Many people heard her, found Jesus, and were born into the family of God.

The third illustration is a story I love. In the ninth chapter of John a blind man encounters Jesus. The disciples are saying that this man is blind because his parents or grandparents did something terrible, but Jesus assures them that is not necessarily the case. After he receives his sight, the religious leaders are upset, claiming that God may have healed him but Jesus did not.

"He answered and said, whether he be a sinner or no, I know not: one thing I know, that, whereas I was blind, now I see" (John 9:25). When Jesus comes in and changes your life, that is exactly what happens – your spiritual blindness is replaced with spiritual sight. This is what it means to be born again. Sainthood is a gift from God. God's grace positions believers as saints.

Colosse was a town in Asia Minor about 100 miles east of Ephesus. Both Greeks and Jews lived there. The Gnostics were a religious group who taught Jesus had not come in the flesh.

Colosse was deserted by 700 A.D. The city today is nothing but ruins. A visitor will find a field of broken structures and mutilated columns. There remains the debris of a cemetery.

The epistle begins with the apostle identifying himself as such and he mentions his fellow-Christian Timotheus. He addresses the fellow workers by the terms 'saints and faithful brethren'. The Greek term 'adelphes' speaks of brethren and every Christian, male or female, is a brother or sister in Christ and it refers to our relationship with the Savior.

The opening verses of Colossians address a most important doctrine, the Trinity. One God is revealed in three persons. There is God the Father, the Son, and the Holy Spirit. The section opens in verse 1 with "the will of God", a reference to the Father. In verse 2, God is 'our Father' and in verse 3 He is the 'Father of our Lord Jesus Christ'. In verse 6, the reference is to "the grace of God in truth" which again is a reference to the Father. In verse 12 we are to thank the Father and in verse 19 it pleased the Father that in Christ all the fullness should dwell. In the Old Testament God is often seen as an omnipotent, holy, and righteous God who knows, sees, and has power over all things. Such an example of this is Psalms 139. In verses 1 through 6 we are introduced to the omniscience of God.

> [1] O Lord, thou hast searched me, and known me.
> [2] Thou knowest my downsitting and mine uprising,
> Thou understandest my thought afar off.
> [3] Thou compassest my path and my lying down,
> And art acquainted with all my ways.
> [4] For there is not a word in my tongue, but lo,
> O Lord, thou knowest it altogether.
> [5] Thou hast beset me behind and before,
> And laid thine hand upon me.
> [6] Such knowledge is too wonderful for me;
> It is high, I cannot attain unto it.

The Lord searches us and knows us. He knows when we sit and rise. He knows our paths and every word on our tongue is known by God before it is spoken. In verses 7 through 12 he is omnipresent.

[7] Whither shall I go from thy spirit?
>   Or whither shall I flee from thy presence?
[8] If I ascend up into heaven, thou art there:
>   If I make my bed in hell, behold, thou art there.
[9] If I take the wings of the morning,
>   And dwell in the uttermost parts of the sea;
[10] Even there shall thy hand lead me,
>   And thy right hand shall hold me.
[11] If I say, Surely the darkness shall cover me;
>   Even the night shall be light about me.
[12] Yea, the darkness hideth not from thee;
>   Aud the night shineth as the day: the darkness
>   And the light are both alike to thee.

There is no way to escape God's presence! Even in Heaven and Hell He is acutely aware and cannot be escaped! In verses 13 to 24 He is omnipotent. He is all powerful.

[13] For thou hast possessed my reins:
>   Thou hast covered me in my mother's womb.
[14] I will praise thee; for I am fearfully and
>   Wonderfully made: marvelous are thy works;
>   And that my soul knoweth right well.
[15] My substance was not hid from thee,
>   When I was made in secret, and curiously
>   Wrought in the lowest parts of the earth.
[16] Thine eyes did see my substance, yet being unperfect;
>   And in thy book all my members were written,
>   Which in continuance were fashioned,
>   When as yet there was none of them.
[17] How precious also are thy thoughts unto me, O God!
>   How great is the sum of them!
[18] If I should count them, they are more in number than
>   The sand: when I awake, I am still with thee.

[19] Surely thou wilt slay the wicked. O God:
>   Depart from me therefore, ye bloody men.

²⁰ For they speak against thee wickedly,
    And thine enemies take thy name in vain.
²¹ Do not I hate them, O Lord, that hate thee? And am
    Not I grieved with those that rise up against thee?
²² I hate them with perfect hatred:
    I count them mine enemies.
²³ Search me, O God, and know my heart:
    Try me, and know my thoughts:
²⁴ And see if there be any wicked way in me,
    And lead me in the way everlasting.

He forms us as we are. We are skillfully and wonderfully made. Because of the omniscience, omnipresence, and omnipotence of God, we can take our anxieties to him and recognize His watching over us.

Some have taken this concept of the character of God and expressed a sense of fear towards God. There is no question that we need to fear God but we can miss out on his loving relationship to us as a Father.

God as a Father is not foreign to the Old Testament. "Have we not all one Father? Has not one God created us?" (Malachi 2:10). "For I am a Father to Israel" (Jeremiah 31:9). Yet few seemed to grasp the Fatherhood of God. Jesus was the one who seemed to emphasize God's fatherhood in clear terms. When he taught us to pray, he said to address God with "Our Father" (Luke 11:1-4). When Jesus rose from the grave, he said to Mary Magdalene, "... touch me not; for I am not yet ascended to my Father: but go to my brethren, and say unto them, I ascend unto my Father, and your Father; and to my God, and your God" (John 20:17). In John 14:28, he addressed the greatness of His Father with, "I am going to the Father; for my Father is greater than I".

God is revealed in His Son. The title of this book, *He Must Be The One!* is a reference to Jesus Christ. The epistle immediately addresses the apostle as an "apostle of Jesus Christ". In verse 2 the Son is named Lord Jesus Christ. This is a very common reference in the Epistles. The word Lord is the Greek word 'Kurios' meaning Master. Jesus refers to His earthly name and that He is Savior. Christ is 'Christos' meaning anointed one or the fulfillment of the Messiah. In verse 6 the gospel is mentioned which refers to the good news of the death, burial, and resurrection of Christ. Epaphras is mentioned as the minister of Christ. The book is full of references to the Son.

In verse 8 the indwelling of the Spirit in Colossians is mentioned and attested to by Epaphras. It is very alarming that in the body of Christ there is such a controversy over the person and work of God the Holy Spirit. Worship wars in churches, the gifts of the spirit, and harboring bitterness, which is the grieving of the spirit (Ephesians 4:30-32), will limit the work of the Holy Spirit (I Thessalonians 5:19). The quenching of the spirit is dousing and putting out the fire of possession in our lives. The spirit is the comforter and encourager for each Christian (John 14:15-18).

The Holy Spirit is normally mentioned last in any discussion of the Trinity; however, it should not be considered that He is inferior in any way to the Father or the Son.

We, therefore, have one God (Deuteronomy 6:4) revealed in three persons with distinct responsibilities. Colossians is a doctrinal book, and the Holy Spirit is primary to the basic teaching of the epistle.

We also need to focus on **fraternity**. This is a word most commonly associated with social organizations for college students. It is defined as a brotherly relationship. Paul speaks in verses 3-6 about the bond we have in Christ.

"We give thanks to God and the Father of our Lord Jesus Christ, praying always for you, since we heard of your faith in Christ Jesus, and of the love which ye have to all the saints, for the hope which is laid up for you in heaven, whereof ye heard before in the word of the truth of the gospel; which is come unto you, as it is in all the world; and bringeth forth fruit, as it doth also in you, since the day ye heard of it, and knew the grace of God in truth."

He talks about the fraternity of the saints and the fraternity of prayer. When you accept Christ, there is a need to find what I call a fraternity of believers. They come from all walks of life and have different ideas about various subjects, but they are always there for you.

All of us need the church. Many people believe that they have no need for the church, but Jesus taught in Matthew 16:18, "*Upon this rock I will build my church, and the gates of hell shall not prevail against it.*"

The church is a fraternity of believers. We need each other, and the longer we live in this world the more we recognize our need for one another.

The people at Colosse learned to love each other. They were not indifferent to the needs of others or critical of the motives of others.

The future, in some ways, is unknown, but our possession is certain. Our faith rests in the past, our love is practiced in the present, and our hope is looking to the future. Paul uses the word "hope" in these verses in Colossians and it carries with it the expectancy of what God has for us in the future.

An important phrase in verse 6 is "*bringeth forth fruit.*" Are you bringing forth fruit today? When you come to the house of God, bring your family and friends. Bring others who need to be in church. As a church we must germinate or we will terminate. The church that does not evangelize will fossilize. This is true in our individual Christian lives as well.

Finally, we see the need to focus on **family**. Verse 7 talks about Epaphras, the faithful pastor at Colosse, and verse 8 shows that he spoke highly of the congregation, as he "*declared unto us your love in the Spirit.*" Not only was the pastor faithful, but so were the people.

There are institutions ordained by God that draw us together. There is the institution of the home and the family, which is really a special place. There is the church, which should be enjoyed by the entire family together. Don't send your children to church; take them with you. If you get involved in a solid local church, you will make some of the greatest friends.

When I was just out of high school I pitched in a men's fast-pitch softball league. I used to go out in the driveway and practice with my father, and I tried to throw it as hard as I could. Some pitches flew ten feet over his head, and he finally told me that I would have to chase the balls that were out of his reach. After several lengthy trips to retrieve the ball, I decided to stay focused. I became a much better pitcher.

I had two different catchers on my team, one named Dave and the other named Gary. Both of them told me the same thing, which was to focus on the catcher's glove. "Don't focus on the batters, the fielders or anything else," each of them said. "Just focus on my glove."

What are we focusing on today? Look at Philippians 4:11-12. *"Not that I speak in respect of want: for I have learned, in whatsoever state I am, therewith to be content. I know both how to be abased, and I know how to abound: every where and in all things I am instructed both to be full and to be hungry, both to abound and to suffer need."*

Paul knew both extremes – to have and have-not. He was born into a family of wealth and privilege, yet he wrote these words while in prison. How does someone live life in contentment? The answer lies in the very next verse: *"I can do all things through Christ which strengtheneth me."*

San Diego pastor David Jeremiah said that we need four things: something to put on (clothes), something to put in (food), something to put up (shelter), and something to put away (money for the future when you cannot work). Those things are important, but beyond that we need the real source of our strength. We need the blessed Trinity.

We need each other, but most of all we need Him. Through faith, fraternity, and family we have a unique blessing to help us get through life. It is good to have a Savior who provides this for us.

Chapter Two

FOCUS ON PRAYER

"For this cause we also, since the day we heard it, do not cease to pray for you, and to desire that ye might be filled with the knowledge of his will in all wisdom and spiritual understanding; that ye might walk worthy of the Lord unto all pleasing, being fruitful in every good work, and increasing in the knowledge of God; strengthened with all might, according to his glorious power, unto all patience and longsuffering with joyfulness; giving thanks unto the Father, which hath made us meet to be partakers of the inheritance of the saints in light." **(Colossians 1:9-12)**

One day I was in a professional building in downtown Miami and as I walked through the lobby, I saw a man at a vending machine. Apparently the machine was not working and he began punching it with his fists, which I know many of us have thought about doing from time to time (I always make sure no one is watching when I do it). He also began shaking and kicking the machine, and as I walked by I heard him utter a few colorful words that certainly are not suitable for this publication. He was extremely upset because he did not get what he wanted.

Sometimes that is our attitude with prayer. We treat God like a vending machine, putting in our requests like coins and expecting a certain response. Often we expect God to do something magically unique and wonderful.

How many times have we prayed and actually found ourselves giving advice to God? We tell Him what He should do, how He should do it, and when it is the best time for Him to do it. We have it all figured out, and we think that if God will just follow our plan it will turn out just great. I don't think God is very impressed with our advice.

Despite our misuse of it, prayer is a great discipline of the Christian life. Oxford author and scholar C.S. Lewis wrote this about prayer: "Prayer, in the sense of petition [asking for things], is a small part of it. Confession and penitence are its threshold, adoration is its sanctuary. The presence, vision, and enjoyment of God is its bread and its wine."

When most of us pray, we pray for things. "Lord, I need money. I need a job. I need healing. I need a family situation settled. An important event is coming up. Give me safety as I go from place to place." Sometimes we pray for vision or prosperity, and often when we pray we cry for help.

You may have heard the story of the child who prayed, "Thank you, Lord, for my baby brother. But I really wanted a puppy!" We are not surprised to hear something like that from children, but we don't expect adults to pray like that.

When I was a young adult I prayed about who I would marry. I told God, "Please show me who the right woman is, and let me know what she looks like before I find her so I won't waste time with anybody else."

Requests often include, "God, take away my cancer," or "Restore my spouse to our home."

When Paul talked about prayer in Colossians, it was not like any of these types of prayers. Prayer is asking but it is much more than that.

Author E. Schulyer English said, "Prayer is surrender. It is surrendering to the will of God and cooperation with that will. If I throw out a boathook from a boat and attach it to the shore, do I pull the shore to me or do I pull myself to the shore? Prayer is not pulling God to my will, but aligning myself to the will of God."

In verses 9-12 we notice the ingredients of this prayer. Paul begins with his desire. He is praying for others, not himself, and his prayer is about spiritual things, not material things. It is interesting that Paul had not even seen these people; he had heard about them from Epaphras, the pastor in Colosse. But he wanted them to *"be filled with the knowledge of his will in all wisdom and spiritual understanding."*

What do we, as parents, pray about concerning our children? When they are younger, we pray for good grades or safety on a bus trip, and these are good things. Do we pray that our children will have the kind of spiritual wisdom that Paul sought for these people he had not even met?

Colossians 2:10 says, *"And ye are complete in him, which is the head of all principality and power."* Paul reminds us that we are complete in Christ. We have no need to go looking for anything else, because what we already have is enough.

Sometimes we feel that because we have been saved for a while, we know everything we need to know. I am reminded of a college freshman who wrote a 10-page paper titled, "The History of the Universe." It is impossible for anyone to cover that topic in 10 pages, especially at that age. That, however, is how so many of us look at life.

God wants us to know Him and His will for our lives. Warren Wiersbe writes, "God is not a distant dictator." As we study and pray, we begin to get filled with who He is. Paul refers in verse 9 to being filled and also in verse 19: *"For it pleased the Father that in him should all fullness dwell."* This is a key truth in the book of Colossians.

Two people have cancer. They are the same age. You pray for God's healing in both situations. One is healed and the other is not. How do you explain that? It is appropriate to ask God for things but there is more to prayer than just asking for them and that is what Paul is teaching us here.

Paul prayed in verse 9 for the people in the church at Colosse to have spiritual wisdom, or insight. The general will of God is for everyone to be saved, sanctified and Spirit-filled, but His specific will is for each of us to get deep into His Word and know what He is telling us individually. He wants us to be filled with the knowledge of His will and who He is.

In verse 10 we see that He wants us to conduct ourselves in the proper way. *"That ye might walk worthy of the Lord unto all pleasing, being fruitful in every good work, and increasing in the knowledge of God."* So we have seen references to our wisdom, our walk and our work. God prepares the worker before He presents the work.

Many years ago I spoke at a series of prophecy conferences that took place three or four times a year. The organizers were good people who loved God and I was honored to be asked to speak. Many people who attended these meetings brought big Bibles and notebooks, and they were very attentive as I spoke.

As I traveled to several of these conferences in different cities, I soon discovered that many of the same people attended. If they considered that the speaker made a mistake they were ready to pounce on them, yet they did little with all of this knowledge. Our faith should be translated into action.

Your faith needs to be seen not only in head knowledge, but in our walk with God. This is vitally important to understand in our prayer life.

Look back at Colossians 1:2. *"To the saints and faithful brethren in Christ which are at Colosse: Grace be unto you, and peace, from God our Father and the Lord Jesus Christ."* The words *"our Father"* remind us of the special relationship we have with God, and that we can go straight to Him in Heaven when we pray. We have direct access to God at any time.

I called my wife the other day and we were speaking on our cell phones when the line went dead. I tried a couple of times to call back and couldn't get through. By the time I finally connected with her, I had forgotten what important thing I was trying to tell her.

Sometimes cell phones and e-mails do not work, but we can always reach our heavenly Father and that connection will always go through. Aren't you glad about that?

When I lived in Pennsylvania, only two hours from the nation's capital, I had a good friend, Bob Billings, who worked for the U.S. Department of Education. He told me he had three tickets for a very important event and I was invited to come. It was a meeting that involved President Ronald Reagan and Vice President George H.W.

Bush. A large number of important people would be there. I said I would be delighted to attend, so Bob gave me the details.

I remember asking him, "Are you sure the president will actually be there? I've heard about events where the president was supposed to come but didn't."

"Don't worry," said Bob. "The president always shows up for this."

"I'll be there."

We met in the city that day and went to the meeting together. We entered a large, palatial hall and everything was beautiful. As I walked through the hall I looked around and it seemed as though everyone who was someone in Washington at that time was there.

After some time of mingling and talking to people, Bob came over and said, "The president will be here about seven o'clock. Let's go over to get close to the podium."

We did that and were soon standing right up front when they brought out the president's podium. I was admiring the seal on the front, but then I noticed that it was the vice president's seal. I thought that perhaps the vice president was going to come out and speak first, and then the president, but that didn't seem to make much sense to me.

"Are you sure the president is going to be here?" I asked Bob again.

"Yes, he always comes to these things."

"Then why is the vice presidential seal on the podium?"

Bob paused and then said, "That means the president is not coming."

As it turned out, there was some kind of crisis going on at that time and the president was not able to attend. I met Vice President Bush, who would later become president. Of course, despite his previous assurances to me, Bob had no control over these matters.

When you pray, you don't go through Gabriel, Michael, Peter, Paul, Mary or a vice president. You have direct access to the God of Heaven, and no crisis or event can change that. Whether you are 10 years of age or 80, you have the same access if you know Christ.

That brings us to the dynamic of prayer, seen in verse 11: *"Strengthened with all might, according to his glorious power, unto all patience and longsuffering with joyfulness."*

There are two words in the New Testament that are translated as "power." One refers to inherent power such as dynamite, while the other, *kratos*, which refers to manifest power of God. If you have a bad temper but stay under control, that is an example of the power of God. We all know how much strength it took for young David to kill Goliath, but perhaps it took just as much strength and courage for him not to do something nasty to Shimei when he was maligning David and calling him all sorts of names.

This passage also speaks about patience, which is endurance when circumstances are difficult. When things get tough, do not quit. It is always too soon to quit. Longsuffering toward people goes hand in hand with patience.

Let me give you five observations about prayer:

Striking answers to prayer often surround conversion. In the eastern world there are many Muslims who are accepting Christ. Unusual things are happening. Stories are being told by good, solid people about events that are taking place, and it is amazing to see what God is doing. This should remind us to be praying regularly for people who need the Lord because these things often happen as a result of people praying.

Prayer is communication with the Almighty. Larry King, the CNN talk-show host, was interviewed by a minister and at one point the subject of prayer came up. Later he asked King if he had any questions.

"Yes," said King. "When you pray, do you really think God heard that prayer?"

That is a good question.

When we get in a prayer group, we have a tendency to say things we want other people in the group to hear. That's not what prayer is all about. It's about talking directly to Almighty God in Heaven and having a relationship with Him.

The biggest battle in our spiritual lives is the prayer battle. We can hear preaching, we can worship, we can read our Bibles – but when it's time to pray it can be really hard to focus.

I can be sitting at home in my chair and my wife asks me to do something. I get up to do it, but as I'm walking through the house I get distracted, and then I forget what I'm supposed to do (although I know I've forgotten something). So I go back to my chair, as if it will remind me what I've forgotten. A little while later my wife asks, "Did you..." and I say, "Oh, that was it." Focus can be difficult. This is true with prayer.

How long should a person pray? Look at John 17 and read the prayer of Jesus in Gethsemane. This is the great prayer of Jesus. Depending upon how fast you read aloud, you can read the entire chapter in a few minutes. Christ was praying about His relationship with the Father, the disciples' relationships with each other, and for everyone else who would ever be saved. He covered all of this in a prayer of only a few minutes.

When the disciples ask, "Lord, teach us to pray," it is interesting that He only gives a few short words, as in Matthew 6:9-13. "*After this manner therefore pray ye: Our Father which art in heaven, hallowed be thy name. Thy kingdom come, thy will be done in earth, as it is in heaven. Give us this day our daily bread. And forgive us our debts, as we forgive our debtors. And lead us not into temptation, but deliver us from evil: For thine is the kingdom, and the power, and the glory, for ever. Amen.*" There is no time limit on prayer.

In II Chronicles 6 we read about a remarkable day for the people of God. The temple was finally built and Solomon is going to give perhaps his most famous speech. That speech is covered in verses 4-11 (maybe two minutes), and his prayer of dedication follows in verses 12-42 (less than ten minutes).

The issue is not how long we pray; it is more important that we simply pray. Don't go on a guilt trip about the amount of time you are committing to prayer. It can be an all-night prayer meeting or a few words you whisper as you go to bed at night, but prayer will be the Christian's greatest battle.

Prayer is to the Father, through the Son, by the Holy Spirit.

Prayer is often driven by our problems instead of our relationship with God. We have a great God and Savior. The Holy Spirit works directly in our lives in a wonderful way. It is worthwhile to cultivate that relationship with God. In the long run, that is what He wants us to get out of our prayer lives.

Look at verse 12 from the first chapter of Colossians. *"Giving thanks unto the Father, which hath made us meet to be partakers of the inheritance of the saints in light."* Notice the emphasis on thanksgiving. Don't give into your problems; every day is a new beginning. James 1:17 says, *"Every good gift and every perfect gift is from above."*

If I asked you to sit down and come up with a list of things to thank God for, you could make a lengthy list. But sometimes we just need to thank God because He is God.

I read an interesting story recently from Sept. 8, 1960. In the town of Elgin, Illinois, a ministerial student named Edward Spencer rescued 17 people after a terrible accident. It damaged his health so severely that he could never go into the ministry.

Not one of those 17 people came back to say thank you.

Jesus healed 10 lepers. Only one returned to thank Him. When we pray, if we say nothing else, we can give thanks to God. He is worth thanking.

The final part of verse 12 refers to our inheritance. As the children of Israel went into Canaan in the Old Testament, it was their inheritance. We also have a Canaan, which is our heavenly inheritance. God has given us so much through Christ, and I want to challenge you to be a person of prayer.

Years ago a family sent their child to one of our Christian schools in south Florida. The father was a lawyer, the mother a writer – wonderful people – and they have since moved to South Carolina.

This little boy was enamored by the sight of me walking by. I don't know what it was about me that captivated him. One day I walked by and saw that he had a wrapped candy bar in his hand. Suddenly he reached up and handed it to me. Almost as soon as he did that and I took it, he stopped looking at me and started looking at the candy bar. I could tell he wanted it back so I handed it to him. He opened it, took a big bite, wrapped it back up and gave it back to me. It was hilarious.

That is what we do with God sometimes. We get what we want and then give Him the rest. It is so difficult at times to remain focused with regard to prayer, but it is one of the greatest joys a Christian can have. Learn to pray, remembering that you are praying to the God of Heaven, and stay focused.

Chapter Three

FOCUS ON LORDSHIP

"Who hath delivered us from the power of darkness, and hath translated us into the kingdom of his dear Son: In whom we have redemption through his blood, even the forgiveness of sins: Who is the image of the invisible God, the firstborn of every creature: For by him were all things created, that are in heaven, and that are in earth, visible and invisible, whether they be thrones, or dominions, or principalities, or powers: All things were created by him, and for him: And he is before all things, and by him all things consist. And he is the head of the body, the church: who is the beginning, the firstborn from the dead; that in all things he might have the pre-eminence. For it pleased the Father that in him should all fullness dwell; and, having made peace through the blood of his cross, by him to reconcile all things unto himself; by him, I say, whether they be things in earth, or things in heaven. And you, that were sometime alienated and enemies in your mind by wicked works, yet now hath he reconciled in the body of his flesh through death, to present you holy and unblameable and unreproveable in his sight: If ye continue in the faith grounded and settled, and be not moved away from the hope of the gospel, which ye have heard, and which was preached to every creature which is under heaven; whereof I Paul am made a minister." **(Colossians 1:13-23)**

W e are in a battle today for truth. People often ask the question: What is absolute truth? For many it does not exist.

We live in an age of postmodern ideology, and the prevailing idea is, "You have your truth, and I have mine. Your truth is all right for you, and mine works for me, so we can all live happily ever after with each other."

The Bible does not teach this principle, but emphasizes the fact that there **is** absolute truth. One plus one equals two – not three, not ten, not 600. There is one president of the United States at any given time, and no more than one. We know that the earth is round. All of these facts represent absolute truth.

People often ask how they can know that there is a God. There is an order to the world as well as the universe. To assume that it all just happened by accident takes unusual faith. Someone had to bring it all into existence.

Anthony Flew, the author and former atheist, recently stated that there must be a Creator because of the design of the universe.

We note the various books that appear each year on the best-seller lists, and they cover a wide range of topics. However, do you realize that 150 million Bibles are printed around the world every year?

There are some great books available now that address the subject of absolute truth, including *The New Evidence That Demands A Verdict* by Josh McDowell and *The Case for Christ* by Lee Strobel.

There are more than 25,000 archaeological finds relating to the Bible, and every one of them confirms the authority of the Word of God.

Our bodies are so complex that it is incomprehensible to argue that we are the products of evolution. Darwin talked about "millions" of transitional forms when examining the fossil record, but not one of those exists today and nearly all of the proposed "missing links" have been disproved.

As we consider the subject of absolute truth, I believe that this passage tells us something about the lordship of Jesus Christ and how we should focus on His lordship and who He is. He is truth! There are many people who do not actually deny Him, but choose to give Him prominence rather than preeminence. I would submit to you that Jesus Christ deserves absolute preeminence in our lives because He is exactly who He claims to be.

David Livingstone, the great missionary statesman of years gone by, made this statement: "All that I am, I owe to Jesus Christ, revealed to me in His divine Book."

Author Chris Lyons put it this way: "Jesus said, 'I love you just the way you are, and I love you too much to let you stay just the way you are.'"

Richard Halverson, the former chaplain of the U.S. Senate, said, "Jesus Christ is God's everything for man's total need."

Let's take a few moments now and focus on the Person of the Lord Jesus Christ. If I knew I were to die in a week and you asked me what I would like to preach on my final Sunday in the pulpit, I would want to preach about Jesus Christ. Are you in love with Jesus today? When you talk about Him, you are talking about absolute, total truth. Notice some truth about Jesus.

He delivered us. Look at verse 13: *"Who hath delivered us from the power of darkness, and hath translated us into the kingdom of his dear Son."* In this verse the word *"delivered"* refers to rescuing someone from danger. Christ has rescued us from the authority of Satan.

There is a place called Hell, and from there many people will one day be sent to the lake of fire, known as Gehenna. Someone may just say, "I don't believe that is true," but it is what Jesus taught, and to deny that fact is to deny the very essence of the teaching of Jesus.

However, God does not want us to go to Hell. As the second half of verse 13 shows us, He has given us a way out and conveyed us into the realm of Jesus Christ, in the same way a person might be deported from one country and sent to another. God wants all people to be in His kingdom one day, and He has done everything He can to make sure that you and I can be there with Him.

Verse 14 explains how this is accomplished. *"In whom we have redemption through his blood, even the forgiveness of sins."* He has redeemed us. To redeem is to release a prisoner through payment of a ransom. In this case the ransom was paid not to Satan, but to God the Father. Jesus accepted and fulfilled all of the demands of the law. He qualifies to deliver you from sin and death.

Go back to Exodus 20 and look at the listing of the Ten Commandments – the law of God that Moses brought down from Mount Sinai. Let's briefly peruse the Commandments.

Here are the first three verses of Exodus 20:1-3. *"And God spake all these words, saying, I am the LORD thy God, which have brought thee out of the land of Egypt, out of the house of bondage. Thou shalt have no other gods before me."*

That very first commandment emphasizes our inability to keep the law. None of us can say we have lived our entire lives putting God first. We are often preoccupied with any of a hundred other things, putting them ahead of God.

Verse 4 says, *"Thou shalt not make unto thee any graven image, or any likeness of any thing that is in heaven above, or that is in the earth beneath, or that is in the water under the earth."* If you have anything in your life other than Christ you are worshipping, the Lord wants you to get rid of it.

Verse 7: *"Thou shalt not take the name of the LORD thy God in vain; for the LORD will not hold him guiltless that taketh his name in vain."* You have probably noticed that angry people do not say, "Oh, Confucius!" No one blurts out the name of Buddha in frustration. It is the name of Jesus that is taken in vain, because Satan does not like Jesus Christ and wants us to blame Him when things go wrong.

The next commandment is mentioned in verse 8. *"Remember the sabbath day, to keep it holy."* The principle is that we are to set aside time specifically for God and worship. It is the Sabbath day principle.

Verse 12 says, *"Honour thy father and thy mother: that thy days may be long upon the land which the LORD thy God giveth thee."* Have you always given your parents the honor and dignity to which they are entitled?

By the time you read verse 13, which says, *"Thou shalt not kill,"* you are probably thinking to yourself, "Finally, here's one I've kept." But Jesus said if you have harbored evil thoughts in your heart against someone, that's the same as murder. The same goes for verse 14 – *"Thou shalt not commit adultery."* If you thought it in your mind, you're guilty!

Verse 15 is self-explanatory: *"Thou shalt not steal."* Then verse 16 says, *"Thou shalt not bear false witness against thy neighbour."* Have you ever gossiped about someone or said something untrue to get back at someone?

The final commandment, in verse 17, is one most of us break all the time. *"Thou shalt not covet thy neighbour's house, thou shalt not covet thy neighbour's wife, nor his manservant, nor his maidservant, nor his ox, nor his ass, nor any thing that is thy neighbour's."*

If you are honest with yourself, you cannot read the Ten Commandments without feeling ashamed. This should make us even more aware of the wonderful work the Lord has done for each of us as illustrated in Colossians 1:13-14. **Forgiveness is not an excuse to sin, but an encouragement toward obedience.** Christ has delivered us, conveyed us, redeemed us, and forgiven us.

You may wonder, "How does He have the right to do all of that? What qualifies Him to do those things?" We see the answer to those questions in this passage from Colossians, which includes a great explanation of who Jesus really is.

Verse 15 says, *"Who is the image of the invisible God, the firstborn of every creature."* The word *"image"* here means a replica. No one has seen God the Father, but many people did see God the Son. When we think of the physical image of God, we should think of Jesus – not a great prophet or teacher or religious leader, but God in human flesh. If you want to know God, you must come to Jesus.

The use of the words *"firstborn"* and *"creature"* in the second half of that verse do not suggest that Christ was a created being. It means that He is first in importance or in rank among everything that has been created. He is one of a kind, and He is in charge of creation as we know it. That is why he is qualified to forgive and redeem you.

I love to read stories about the antics of Yogi Berra, the legendary catcher for the New York Yankees who played in an astonishing 14 World Series (still a major-league record) and was on the winning team for ten of those. He is well-known today for colorful phrases and statements that do not always make sense but always make people laugh.

In 1957 and 1958 the Yankees squared off against the Milwaukee Braves, whose lineup included a very young outfielder named Henry Aaron. No one knew at the time that Aaron would become arguably the greatest home run hitter ever.

Aaron stepped to the plate in a World Series game and Berra, who was a veteran some ten years older, tried to intimidate him. "You have the bat turned the wrong way," he said. "You can't hit like that."

Unmoved by that comment, Aaron promptly drove the ball into the seats for a home run. As he touched home plate after rounding the bases, he said, "Yogi, I didn't come up here to read the bat. I came up to hit." Aaron's actions at the plate proved his point.

Jesus qualifies because of what He did for us. He died, was buried and rose again.

Look at verses 16-17 to see more of His record. "*For by him were all things created, that are in heaven, and that are in earth, visible and invisible, whether they be thrones, or dominions, or principalities, or powers: all things were created by him, and for him. And he is before all things, and by him all things consist.*"

Philosophy teaches that everything has a primary cause, an instrumental cause and a final cause. Jesus spoke it, practiced it and did it – He fulfilled it all. He created the world and is the sustainer who holds together all of those things He spoke into existence. Jesus is not just some wishful idea, but is the living, eternal Son of God.

Look at verse 18. "*And he is the head of the body, the church: who is the beginning, the firstborn from the dead; that in all things he might have the preeminence.*" Your church has a pastor and staff to oversee its various programs, but we must never forget who is the leader of the church, both locally and universally – our Lord and Savior, Jesus Christ. He bought the church and claimed it with His own blood.

With all of this in mind, let's go back to our discussion about absolute truth. Is Jesus one of the many ways to God? Is He just one of a number of ideas people may have about God? Or is He the only way?

The answer to those questions can be found in John 14:6. "*Jesus saith unto him, I am the way, the truth, and the life: no man cometh unto the Father, but by me."* That is absolute truth, regardless of whether you believe it.

There have been numerous attempts to prove that Jesus is not who He says He is. There are the stories circulating today about Jesus having been married to Mary Magdalene and having relationships with other women. But if you study history and read what His contemporaries had to say, there is no mention of such heresy.

The fact is that Jesus Christ is the Lord of everything, and we need to make Him our Lord as well.

Read these words from Philippians 2:5-8. *"Let this mind be in you, which was also in Christ Jesus: Who, being in the form of God, thought it not robbery to be equal with God: But made himself of no reputation, and took upon him the form of a servant, and was made in the likeness of men: And being found in fashion as a man, he humbled himself, and became obedient unto death, even the death of the cross."*

Jesus set aside some of His divine attributes when He came to earth. He did not have to do that. He could have stopped everything that was happening to Him on the cross. He could have done anything He wanted to do at any time, but He did not because He had to die for the sins of the world.

Now look at the next three verses: *"Wherefore God also hath highly exalted him, and given him a name which is above every name: That at the name of Jesus every knee should bow, of things in heaven, and things in earth, and things under the earth; and that every tongue should confess that Jesus Christ is Lord, to the glory of God the Father"* (Philippians 2:9-11).

One day everyone will have to give an account to Jesus Christ. That is absolute truth. Many choose not to believe it, but that does not change absolute truth, and they will also stand before Him one day and acknowledge His lordship.

Back in Colossians 1, verses 19-23 speak of His reconciling work. This is a beautiful passage.

Verse 20 says, *"For it pleased the Father that in him should all fullness dwell."* The word *"fullness"* denotes that the sum total of all divine power and attributes can be found in God Himself, and the word *"dwell"* says that this is part of His essential being.

So how can a holy God reconcile sinful people? According to verses 20-21, "*And, having made peace through the blood of his cross, by him to reconcile all things unto himself; by him, I say, whether they be things in earth, or things in heaven. And you, that were sometime alienated and enemies in your mind by wicked works, yet now hath he reconciled.*"

This is accomplished, as verse 20 points out, through the blood of Christ. When God looks at you He sees a sinner, He cannot allow you into His presence. But it is wonderful to always remember that once you come to Christ, when God looks at you He sees the blood of Christ that has cleansed your sin. It is not the church or some emotional experience in your life that accomplishes this. It is Jesus and Him alone. Then God looks at you and is pleased, as if you never committed a sin in your life.

Study any famous religious leader from history and you will not find in his life what you find in Jesus. We have already seen that everyone will bow before Him some day, but consider this solemn passage from Revelation 20:11-12.

"*And I saw a great white throne, and him that sat on it, from whose face the earth and the heaven fled away; and there was found no place for them. And I saw the dead, small and great, stand before God; and the books were opened: and another book was opened, which is the book of life: and the dead were judged out of those things which were written in the books, according to their works.*"

The "*dead*" in this passage refers to those who are dead spiritually. This is not annihilation, but separation.

Those who have settled things with Christ on this side of eternity will not experience this, but these who are spiritually dead are being judged by their works because if you have not allowed Jesus to take away your sins, there must be some other way to judge whether you belong in Heaven. The only other way is your works, and we know that our works will not save us.

Continue reading in verses 13-15. "*And the sea gave up the dead which were in it; and death and hell delivered up the dead which were in them: and they were judged every man according to their works. And death and hell were cast into the lake of fire. This is the second death. And whosoever was not found written in the book of life was cast into the lake of fire."*

We all make mistakes. We drive too fast and get speeding tickets. The other day my wife sent me to the store to get eight or nine items and I came back home with only two of them. That is a minor mistake and it can be remedied easily. However, missing out on salvation is a mistake you do not want to make, and you will also want to tell your friends not to make that same mistake. We are sinners in need of a Savior and cannot make the mistake of missing out on salvation.

Spurgeon wrote, "Do you want arguments for soul winning? Look up through Heaven and ask yourself how sinners can ever reach those harps of gold and learn those everlasting songs unless there is someone to tell them about Jesus, who is mighty to save. But the best argument can be found in the wounds of Jesus. You want to honor Him, to put many crowns upon His head, and this you can best do by winning souls for Him. These are the spoils that He covets, these are the trophies for which He fights, these are the jewels for which He is most adorned."

If people are going to Hell, we should get in their way and try to stop them. We need to tell them that Jesus is the one and only way, and there is not another.

The last part of this section of scripture, verses 24-29, remind us of our response to Him. In verse 25 he talks about being a steward, while verses 26-27 refer to a mystery.

In the Bible, a mystery is not something scary but rather a sacred secret. In this case the secret was that God would be bringing Jews and Gentiles into the family of God. Paul was in jail because he preached to the Gentiles. He was not complaining about being in jail, but he knew that was where God wanted him to be at that time.

Look at his words in verse 28: *"Whom we preach, warning every man, and teaching every man in all wisdom; that we may present every man perfect in Christ Jesus."*

There is an old hymn that says, "My Jesus, I love thee, I know thou are mine." The great truth of the Bible is that Jesus Christ absolutely is the Lord.

Here are the words of an African martyr before he died: "I am part of the unashamed. The dye has been cast. I have stepped over the line. The decision has been made. I am a disciple of Jesus Christ. I won't look back, let up, slow down, back away or be still. My past is redeemed, my present makes sense, and my future is secure. I am finished and done with low living, sight-walking, small planning, smooth knees, colorless dreams, tame visions, mundane talking, cheap giving and dwarfed goals. My pace is set. My gate is fast. My goal is Heaven. My road is narrow. My way is tough, my companions may be few, but my guide is reliable. My mission is clear. I won't give up, I won't back up, I won't let up or shut up until I've preached up, prayed up, paid up, stored up and stayed up for the cause of Christ. I must go until He returns, give until I drop, preach until all know and work until He comes. And when He comes to get His own, He'll have no problem recognizing me. My colors will be clear. I am not ashamed of the gospel of Christ."

Karl Barth traveled the world lecturing, and when he came back to his homeland in America he was asked, "What is the greatest truth that you know?"

He replied, "The greatest truth I know is that Jesus loves me, this I know, for the Bible tells me so."

Everyone needs to hear this message. The truth is in Jesus and Jesus alone!

Chapter Four

FOCUS ON PURPOSE

"Who now rejoice in my sufferings for you, and fill up that which is behind of the afflictions of Christ in my flesh for his body's sake, which is the church: Whereof I am made a minister, according to the dispensation of God which is given to me for you, to fulfill the word of God; even the mystery which hath been hid from ages and from generations, but now is made manifest to his saints: To whom God would make known what is the riches of the glory of this mystery among the Gentiles; which is Christ in you, the hope of glory: Whom we preach, warning every man, and teaching every man in all wisdom; that we may present every man perfect in Christ Jesus: Whereunto I also labour, striving according to his working, which worketh in me mightily." **(Colossians 1:24-29)**

Why are we here? If this were your last day on this planet, will you have fulfilled the purpose for your life?

As he wrote these words in Colossians, the Apostle Paul was suffering in jail because he had been preaching to the Gentiles. Instead of reacting bitterly, he built better relationships with a number of people, including those in the city of Colosse. He dealt in this passage with why he was where he was and how that affects all of us.

Notice in verse 24 how that, despite all Paul is going through, he is rejoicing in the Lord. *"Who now rejoice in my sufferings for you, and fill up that which is behind of the afflictions of Christ in my flesh for his body's sake, which is the church.*"

It is interesting to note that the apostle was in prison for the cause of Christ and rejoiced about it. Acts 5:41 says that the apostles were "*rejoicing that they were counted worthy to suffer shame for his name.*"

Paul was jailed on false charges. He took a stand for Christ, proclaimed the gospel to the Gentiles and promoted the church, the body of Christ.

When your life has purpose, you can rejoice in the Lord. Are you rejoicing in the Lord today?

In verses 25-27 we find that he is faithful to the calling that God has given to him. Paul could have spared himself a lot of suffering if he had not been faithful to his calling.

If you do not serve the Lord, the devil will not be interested in attacking you. Satan will not like it, however, if you choose to serve God. Sometimes when we are most content – when things seem to be calm, cool and collected – it may be because we are not serving Him as we should. Paul made it very clear that God had commissioned him and was very involved in his life.

Verse 26 says, "*Even the mystery which hath been hid from ages and from generations, but now is made manifest to his saints.*"

I Peter 1:10-12 helps us understand this verse. "*Of which salvation the prophets have enquired and searched diligently, who prophesied of the grace that should come unto you: Searching what, or what manner of time the Spirit of Christ which was in them did signify, when it testified beforehand the sufferings of Christ, and the glory that should follow. Unto whom it was revealed, that not unto themselves, but unto us they did minister the things, which are now reported unto you by them that have preached the gospel unto you with the Holy Ghost sent down from heaven; which things the angels desire to look into.*"

In the Old Testament we have teachings of the sufferings of Christ. According to this passage it looks like the glory of Christ immediately follows the suffering of Christ, but that is not the case. In reality, the suffering is followed by at least a 2,000-year period we know as the church age, after which is the coming of our Lord. That is what is called the mystery.

As previously mentioned in chapter three, a mystery in the Bible is not something that is eerie or scary, but it refers to a sacred secret that God has revealed. In this case we have the nation of Israel which was called by God to be His people. He gave them the law, the priesthood, the sacrifices of the land. He promised them a king. The Old Testament prophets wrote about a Messiah who would one day suffer.

Now the Jew and the Gentile are coming together in the body of Christ. In fact, Isaiah 49:6 gives an indication of the Messiah's importance in the Gentile world: "*And he said, It is a light thing that thou shouldest be my servant to raise up the tribes of Jacob, and to restore the preserved of Israel: I will also give thee for a light to the Gentiles, that thou mayest be my salvation unto the end of the earth.*" Jews and Gentiles being called together in the church age – that is the mystery Paul is speaking of. It is a reminder to us that we should never lose the love that God gave us through Jesus Christ.

For several months I flew from South Florida, where I was pastoring, to Davis College in upstate New York, where I serve as the president. The airport in Binghamton is small. I was sitting in the terminal one day looking at the plane I would soon be boarding and felt negative emotion because a little plane like this often gets caught in air pockets.

Two small children came running over and were right in front of me when they pointed at the plane and shouted, "There it is! There it is!" This was to be their first-ever airplane ride. Not only that, it was also the first for their mother and father. I saw the dad sitting in a chair looking terrified.

When we boarded, the children jumped into the first two open seats even though they weren't the ones assigned to them. They were so excited. When we first come to Christ there is a sense of exhilaration. Do you still have that love and excitement you once had for Jesus? Don't ever fall out of love with Jesus Christ. Even when you go through tough times, Jesus is still worth loving and following.

Notice in verses 28-29 that He cares about believers. Verse 28 says, "*Whom we preach, warning every man, and teaching every man in all wisdom; that we may present every man perfect in Christ Jesus.*"

Occasionally we all fall into a habit of followings rules and regulations. Paul writes in Colossians 2:16 "*Let no man therefore judge you in meat, or in drink, or in respect of a holy day, or of the new moon, or of the sabbath days.*" He states further in verses 20-22, "*Wherefore if ye be dead with Christ from the rudiments of the world, why, as though living in the world, are ye subject to ordinances, (touch not; taste not; handle not; which all are to perish with the using;) after the commandments and doctrines of men?*"

He is telling us something very important here. The Bible teaches us about living a holy life, but also about not living a legalistic life because we miss out on so much about what the Savior has done for us.

Jesus has a purpose for your life. Why are we here? Are you living in God's purpose for your life? Those are the questions we must consider. Here are five ideas from these verses that I think will help us understand life's purpose.

Life's purpose is best learned during suffering. I wish this would not be true.

We can understand Paul's writing in Colossians somewhat better by looking back at why he was in prison. Read Acts 22:21-24. "*And he said unto me, depart: for I will send thee far hence unto the Gentiles. And they gave him audience unto this word, and then lifted up their voices, and said, away with such a fellow from the earth: for it is not fit that he should live. And as they cried out, and cast off their clothes, and threw dust into the air, the chief captain commanded him to be brought into the castle, and bade that he should be examined by scourging; that he might know wherefore they cried so against him.*"

Paul learned lessons in jail that he would never learn on the mountaintop.

When Jesus took Peter, James and John up to the Mount of Transfiguration, Peter suggested that they build temples and enjoy that special spot, but Christ pointed out that they were not there for that reason.

When we are in the valley, we have to ask ourselves, "How do I get out of here?" This is usually the time when God is instructing us in something important.

I have a series of letters from a woman I led to Christ several years ago. She did something wrong and was incarcerated, and she wrote me from jail. In her last letter to me she stated that she believed she had found God's purpose for her life. I would not recommend that you take this course of action, but it is interesting that she learned a life lesson in prison.

Recently I talked to a man who had been without a job for an entire year. He was absolutely a bitter man, even though he had found a new job. I predict he will not go far in life unless he changes the way he reacts to the things that happen to him.

The purpose of life is best learned when you are going through the gymnasium of suffering – when you are going through the moments of life you wish were not there. I would not recommend asking God to lead you into suffering so you can find your purpose, but I would say that as you go through suffering, affliction or loss, God will begin to reveal Himself to you.

Life's purpose is absolutely specific. I do not believe in the idea that the will of God could be any of a number of things. When you accept Christ there are a number of good things you could do, but I believe that God's will is a specific thing.

God called Abraham and told him to look for a land. He did not call Moses or Isaac. God called Moses to take the stone tablets with the Ten Commandments down from the mountain. He did not call anyone else.

God called Joshua to take the children of Israel into the Promised Land and Saul (later Paul) to take the Gospel to the Gentiles. God's will for each of us is specific, and we should pray to that end.

When I was in high school, our youth pastor Paul Blasko said that all of the young men should pray that God lead us to the right person to marry. I thought that was good advice and began to pray for that. I even asked God to let me know what she would look like so I wouldn't waste my time with anyone else.

I remember the first time I saw the woman who would later become my wife. She was not sure about me, but we eventually married and I was so glad my youth pastor had given me that advice.

John went to Patmos. Philip went to the Samaritans. Thomas went to India. God's will is specific.

Finding life's purpose is a gradual unveiling. Ecclesiastes 3:1 says, *"To every thing there is a season, and a time to every purpose under the heaven."* It would be great if God would just say, "Here is everything I want you to know for the rest of your life." He doesn't operate that way. There are no shortcuts with God.

Sometimes we do not think the way He wants us to think, or we think we know what is best but God has something totally different in store for us. When we step back and take a good look, we see what God is really doing.

With the book of Malachi, the Old Testament is brought to an end. There was no new revelation from God for 400 years, which we call the silent years. But, as Galatians 4:4 tells us, *"when the fullness of the time was come, God sent forth his Son."*

I am convinced that God leads and directs us in life through a gradual process, and sometimes we learn things that are not as they should be. Sometimes we have to "unlearn" some things, as there are no magic pills or even principles that will allow us to undo the damage of past years. All of your faults, failures and hang-ups may be there, but as you continue to grow, character is built into your life. After a while you will see that God is slowly unveiling to you His plan.

The book of James tells us – and I paraphrase here – not to try to get out of anything prematurely, but to work through it, so you can become mature and better developed. D.L. Moody once said, "The Bible was not given to us to increase our knowledge, but to change our lives." So often we look at culture or logic or some other thing, and we forget that spiritual growth is vital in our lives. You must want to grow, decide to grow, and affect your life so that you will grow. The fourth chapter of Ephesians says that we are to grow more like Christ in everything and not remain as children.

God wants us to mature and uses everything for our good. He wants us to understand that we are to follow His purpose and plan for our lives. It is a slow, gradual unveiling.

You do not feed a newborn baby a hot dog during its first week of life. You do not give a five-year-old access to the oven. Just as a parent is careful with a child, God takes special care with us as we worship Him and look to Him. Sometimes His purpose takes us to places or shows us things we never imagined.

So let me ask you again: If this were your last day alive, how would you be doing with what God has given you?

Your life's purpose will always involve others. Go back to the beginning of Colossians and you will see that Paul mentions "*you*," "*ye*" or "*your*" a total of 15 times in the first 10 verses but not a single "*I*" or "*me*." He is thinking continually about others.

When we come to Christ we become part of the family of God. Everyone who is a follower of Jesus Christ must understand the need to become part of a body of believers known as the local church. We gather corporately to worship and hear the teaching of the Word of God, and we must be involved steadily in the local church. It is there that we find the people we need in life.

You can find purpose, people, principles to live by, and power for your life in the local church. We have fellowship by experiencing life together, and I want to challenge you to get to know people in the house of the Lord.

In finding life's purpose you will create your legacy. This is what you will become and what you will leave behind. There are no shortcuts to growth and maturity. While we concern ourselves with how fast we might grow, God is concerned with how strong we will grow. As you live your life for Him, you find that you will leave to others what they need to have to make themselves strong. You will make a difference in other people's lives.

I received a letter recently from a man who was in our church youth group and Christian school many years ago in Pennsylvania. He found himself often in the principal's office in those days, and once he came to my office and explained to me why he thought I should fire the principal.

Now he is the pastor of a church and leads a great congregation. In his letter he thanked me for the input I had into his life, and I thought to myself, "That is really what life is all about."

Your life is not to be lived in a vacuum unto yourself. It's not just about what pleases or benefits "me, myself and I." It is about making a difference in other people, especially those who will be following you.

So if this were the end of your life, if today were the final day, what are you leaving behind? When you consider that question, it makes all the difference as far as why you are here at this moment in time.

How are you making your family the best it can be? How are you impacting your church and making it better? What is your influence in your neighborhood, your workplace or your city? Where is God directing you and how is He leading you?

Having that kind of purpose is absolutely vital for living out your life. When it's all said and done, we can say it was well worth it because we have left a legacy.

An elderly lady, in a church I attended as a child, would go to the tract rack and take as many tracts as her purse could hold. People were amused as she went to the bus station and handed them to people getting off the bus, or distributed them in any location where people gathered. Some folks laughed at her, but she led more people to Christ in a year than most preachers would in a lifetime. She was doing what she felt God would have her do.

Her pastor came to her once and asked, "Why are you taking all of the tracts? There aren't any left for other people in the church to take."

She responded with a question of her own. "Do the other people pass them out?"

"I don't know."

"Well, pastor, I can promise you this: I pass out every tract I get. If I think a person is already a Christian, I take it back. I try to pass them out to people who do not know Jesus. That is my purpose."

When you start to realize your purpose, you want to get up in the morning. The Apostle Paul suffered in jail for the cause of Christ, because he preached to the Gentiles, but he knew his purpose and that allowed him to rejoice in his suffering. Only Jesus Christ could do that in someone's life.

I knew a lady named Anna who was an invalid. She could not get out of bed. Every time I went to visit her, she encouraged me more than I could ever encourage her.

"Pastor," she told me one day, "my purpose is to bless everyone who comes to see me." What a blessing she was.

The average lifespan today is around 80 years of age. Where are you on that scale? The fact is you don't know when your time on this earth will be over. Whatever your stage in life, you need to be working to fulfill the purpose God has given you, and you need to start today.

Chapter Five

FOCUS ON MATURITY

"For I would that ye knew what great conflict I have for you, and for them at Laodicea, and for as many as have not seen my face in the flesh; that their hearts might be comforted, being knit together in love, and unto all riches of the full assurance of understanding, to the acknowledgement of the mystery of God, and of the Father, and of Christ; in whom are hid all the treasures of wisdom and knowledge. And this I say, lest any man should beguile you with enticing words. For though I be absent in the flesh, yet am I with you in the spirit, joying and beholding your order, and the stedfastness of your faith in Christ. As ye have therefore received Christ Jesus the Lord, so walk ye in him: Rooted and built up in him, and stablished in the faith, as ye have been taught, abounding therein with thanksgiving. Beware lest any man spoil you through philosophy and vain deceit, after the tradition of men, after the rudiments of the world, and not after Christ. For in him dwelleth all the fullness of the Godhead bodily. And ye are complete in him, which is the head of all principality and power." **(Colossians 2:1-10)**

My wife recently celebrated a birthday. We have a birthday tradition in our home in which the honoree sits in a special chair to receive gifts. The grandchildren were present for this particular celebration, and they jumped into Grandma's lap with excitement because they knew the gifts were coming and that she would let them open the gifts.

If I were to walk over, sit on the arm of the chair and start opening my wife's gifts, you might ask about my motive. I am an adult. However, it is perfectly acceptable for a child to do that because children have not yet reached the level of maturity that adults have (or should have) reached.

With that in mind, I want you to think for a moment about your maturity level as a child of God. It's one thing to be born again, but one's growth in the Lord after salvation that is another issue entirely.

Look at I Thessalonians 5:23. "*And the very God of peace sanctify you wholly; and I pray God your whole spirit and soul and body be preserved blameless unto the coming of our Lord Jesus Christ.*"

This is a very interesting thought from the Apostle Paul concerning growth in the Lord. Often we talk about the concept of body, soul and spirit. This verse reverses that order.

We place a great deal of emphasis on caring for our bodies, whether it is through diet, exercise or general health care. The soul is often referred to as the personality or the "you" that you are, but the spirit is the part of us that has a personal relationship with God. I can relate to you through my body or soul, but through my spirit I relate to God. Understanding this principle can help us see why Paul listed spirit, soul and body in that order.

Things in our everyday lives, and especially people, can bother us or get to us in a negative way affecting our body and soul, but the things that affect the spirit are the deep things of God. It would be good to ask yourself how deep you are right now in your walk with God.

The word "*rooted*" in verse 7 is the key word for the entire second chapter of Colossians. It refers to the part of a plant that is in position below the ground. It is an agricultural term. The plant draws water and nourishment from the soil and also stores food. From this application we have expanded the use of the word "root" to refer to the source or origin of a specific action.

If you are rooted in the Lord, you are not going to be blown away. These passages suggest to us that we are to be rooted in Him and involved with Him through spirit, soul and body. The Spirit of God working in us will build us in the Christian faith.

Notice that the affairs of our daily lives will often make it difficult for us to remain rooted as we should. As we examine the signs of maturity that are displayed in these verses, we should ask ourselves if our lives reflect the kind of maturity that is being urged here.

One sign of maturity is **a life of intercession**. Paul writes in Colossians 2:1-5 of going deep into the things of God through prayer.

Look at verse 1. "*For I would that ye knew what great conflict I have for you, and for them at Laodicea, and for as many as have not seen my face in the flesh.*"

The word "*conflict*" depicts a struggle or exertion. It is actually a picture of a Greek runner competing in something akin to our Olympic Games. Often our prayers can be very calm and easy, but there are times in our prayer lives when we need to get close to God and agonize with Him about events that are taking place.

We should be like that runner who does everything he can to prevail in the race. It can be likened to wrestling with God, but not in a combative sense. Prayer is the task of finding the mind of God, not changing the mind of God. As we learn the mind of God, He begins to put certain desires in us.

Prayer is not just saying, "Lord, bless me today. Help me today. Give me money today." It is something that should first be done on behalf of others, as Paul himself demonstrates in these verses. Intercession is a sign of maturity.

Verse 2 shows that this is also meant to comfort believers. "*That their hearts might be comforted, being knit together in love, and unto all riches of the full assurance of understanding, to the acknowledgement of the mystery of God, and of the Father, and of Christ.*"

If you are maturing in the Lord, you will be an encourager to other people. We all know people who are discouragers. No one wants to spend time with discouraging people, but encouragers elicit the opposite response. When you are an encourager, people will want to be around you and unsaved people will want what you have in your life.

Look at how Christ is described in verse 3. "*In whom are hid all the treasures of wisdom and knowledge.*" Jesus Christ is the source of all answers for life, because He is wisdom. The word "*treasures*" in this verse comes from the same word that gives us the English word "thesaurus." It is a place of safekeeping, where we can find all of the wisdom of Almighty God.

We often measure our maturity by the way we behave, the things we do or don't do, and the places we go or don't go. Real maturity, however, is measured by the depth of our relationship with the Lord Jesus Christ.

There is a warning in verse 4: "*And this I say, lest any man should beguile you with enticing words.*" This phrase actually contains a legal term that describes the persuasion of a lawyer – someone with a sharp mind who speaks exceptionally well – and it is used to warn us especially about deceivers.

The fact that someone may persuade you does not make it true. What we regard as truth must be compared with the authority of the Word of God. In Paul's day a group known as the Gnostics were working hard to convince people that the Messiah had not yet come in the flesh, and Paul felt it necessary to warn others so they were not deceived. In our day, as in Paul's, the Bible must be our guide.

He writes in verse 5, "*For though I be absent in the flesh, yet am I with you in the spirit, joying and beholding your order, and the steadfastness of your faith in Christ.*" The words "*order*" and "*steadfastness*" are military terms that denote one's duty assignment and a solid front against the enemy.

We are regularly engaged in spiritual warfare. Every day that you desire to live for Jesus Christ, the devil will fight against you. Our enemy is very real and powerful, and he will do everything he can do to stop you from serving the Lord. The best thing you can do is tell the devil to go back where he came from and remind him of the victory we have through the cross of Christ.

Another sign of maturity, shown in verses 5-6, is **a life of exhortation**.

"*Christ*" is the anointed One – the Messiah – and "*Jesus*" means "savior," but the word "*Lord*" is especially important here because it means that He is the absolute master of your life. You will never reach the right level of maturity as a Christian until you decide once and for all that Jesus Christ is the Lord of your life. When you acknowledge His lordship, you will grow in your walk with Him.

The word "*walk*" is a key word. Colossians 1:10 says, "*That ye may walk worthy of the Lord.*" That refers to our Christian conduct. There are other instances where we see this.

In the which ye also walked sometime, when ye lived in them. (Colossians 3:7)

Walk in wisdom toward them that are without, redeeming the time. (Colossians 4:5)

We also read the word "*walk*" several times in the book of Ephesians. All of these passages emphasize going on and forward in the things of God.

The Gnostics of Paul's day were a religious sect who insisted that Jesus had come only as a spirit, but Paul stressed that this was not the case. He taught that Jesus had come in the flesh. The issue in our day and age is whether Jesus Christ is really God.

If He were not God, then He could not save. He could not be the Creator. Many people claim that He was only a prophet or a good man, but the Bible teaches that Jesus Christ is God in human flesh. The Son of God has always been in existence, but He became a man in the form of Jesus of Nazareth, who lived on Earth for 33 years, died, was buried, and rose again. The fact is that Jesus is God. Notice the scriptural testimonies.

God the Father, speaking in Hebrews 1:8 about His own Son, said, "*But unto the Son he saith, Thy throne, O God, is for ever and ever: a sceptre of righteousness is the sceptre of thy kingdom.*"

John 1:1 says, "*In the beginning was the Word, and the Word was with God, and the Word was God.*"

Mary, knowing that she would give birth to the Son of God, said in Luke 1:47, "*And my spirit hath rejoiced in God my Savior.*"

Jesus was called God by His heavenly Father as well as His earthly mother. There is no doubt that He is God in the flesh.

As we mature in Christ, we establish the characteristics of Christ so that we can build our lives in Him as illustrated in verse 7. "*Rooted and built up in him, and stablished in the faith, as ye have been taught, abounding therein with thanksgiving.*" While "*rooted*" is an agricultural term as we discussed earlier, "*stablished*" is an architectural or construction term. This illustrates that we are to have a solid foundation in Him that will not be easily moved.

Verse 8 says, "*Beware lest any man spoil you through philosophy and vain deceit, after the tradition of men, after the rudiments of the world, and not after Christ.*" This passage urges us to keep our eyes on Jesus, and as we watch Him work in our lives we can move on to excellence through Him.

The third sign of maturity is **knowledge of what Christ is in us**. Verse 9 points out, "*For in him dwelleth all the fullness of the Godhead bodily.*"

There is much discussion in today's Christian society on how to "grow a church." What are some of the methods for doing that? There are several ways to grow, such as attracting disgruntled members of other churches and new residents in the community. It can even be done by existing members having babies.

The church of Jesus Christ is not supposed to grow primarily by those methods, but rather by conversion growth – people accepting Christ, following Him in believer's baptism and then being discipled in the things of God. Paul is talking about precisely that in verse 9, after reminding us in verse 8 about those who would destroy the faith of some believers through false teaching.

Suppose I placed two glasses of water on your kitchen table. One contains pure, clear water. The other contains the same kind of water and also has a worm in it. Which one will you want to drink?

Just as you would prefer water in its purest form, so should you desire only the pure teaching and doctrine of Christ as taught in the Word of God. We need to see others come to the same knowledge of Christ that we have, and part of your maturity is shown when you help others see their lives changed by the power of the Gospel.

Look at verse 10. "*And ye are complete in him, which is the head of all principality and power.*" He is all you will ever need, and through Him you are full. It is not Jesus plus the law, or your works, or your church denomination. It is Jesus alone.

The church I pastored in Florida hosted Dr. Harold Peasley, a Christian leader from South Africa, for a Wednesday night Bible study. He gave a great message that included the following story.

Reverend Francis Dixon was conducting a testimony service at his church in England when a young man named Peter rose to speak. Peter testified he was walking down George Street in Sydney Australia one Sunday night when a man came from out of nowhere and spoke to him.

"I would like to say a few words to you," the man said courteously. "I hope you are not offended. Do you know where you will live in eternity – Heaven or Hell? It is a very important matter. That is all. Good night."

The man was on his way as mysteriously as he had appeared.

"I thought often about that question, so when I returned to England I sought out someone who could help me," said Peter. "It was that man on George Street who started me on my way to Christ."

A few weeks after this testimony service, Reverend Dixon arranged for a mission team to visit his church. A young man named Noel from that group gave his testimony.

"I was stationed in Sydney while serving in the armed forces," he said. "One day while walking down George Street, a man came out of the shadows and spoke to me." It was the same brief statement about eternity that Peter had received, and Noel acknowledged that those words moved him to see his need for Christ.

After that service, Peter approached Noel and told him they shared the same testimony. They wondered who this mysterious man might be.

A short time later Dixon made his first trip to Australia. While speaking in a church there, he told the story of Peter and Noel. A man in the congregation interrupted and asked if he could give a testimony. He told of the same thing happening to him on George Street in Sydney.

Dixon included this in a later sermon in Perth, on the western end of Australia, and a deacon in that church said he had the same testimony. When he returned to England to report on his trip, he mentioned all of these episodes and heard from yet another person who had the same encounter. This continued as Dixon spoke at a subsequent conference and on trips to India and Jamaica.

Finally, he made a trip to Sydney and asked a man if he happened to know the identity of this mysterious man on George Street.

"Yes, I know him," he replied. "His name is Frank Jenner."

He agreed to take Dixon to a suburb of Sydney to meet Jenner, who was by this time an old man and very ill. After entering the small cottage where Jenner lived, Dixon was introduced to this unknown man who so often spoke of eternity.

Dixon told of the eight people he had met all over the world with the same testimony from George Street. Tears came to Jenner's eyes.

"I don't know how many times I walked that street and spoke to people about eternity," Jenner said. "This is the first time I have heard of anyone coming to Christ."

In the years to come, Jenner's life was researched more thoroughly and it was determined that a quarter-million people came to Christ as a result of this man's efforts. Little did he know what kind of impact he would have.

It is unlikely that Frank Jenner was involved in gossip or criticism to a great extent during his life, because he didn't have time for such things. He had a singular pursuit, and that was spreading the Gospel. This is a sign of a mature Christian life.

When we begin to mature in the Lord, He begins to work in our lives and we want to live our lives for Him and serve Him; we want to be the best that we can possibly be for the glory of God. Like Paul, who wrote these passages while in prison, we need to do whatever we can amid our own circumstances to live our lives for Christ. It will always be well worth doing.

There is a fulfillment and joy that comes from living to the fullest in the faith that God has given to you. It is a wonderful thing to move forward continually and grow in the things of God.

Chapter Six

FOCUS ON FREEDOM

"In whom also ye are circumcised with the circumcision made without hands, in putting off the body of the sins of the flesh by the circumcision of Christ: Buried with him in baptism, wherein also ye are risen with him through the faith of the operation of God, who hath raised him from the dead. And you, being dead in your sins and the uncircumcision of your flesh, hath he quickened together with him, having forgiven you all trespasses; blotting out the hand-writing of ordinances that was against us, which was contrary to us, and took it out of the way, nailing it to his cross; and having spoiled principalities and powers, he made a shew of them openly, triumphing over them in it. Let no man therefore judge you in meat, or in drink, or in respect of an holyday, or of the new moon, or of the sabbath days: Which are a shadow of things to come; but the body is of Christ. Let no man beguile you of your reward in a voluntary humility and worshipping of angels, intruding into those things which he hath not seen, vainly puffed up by his fleshly mind, and not holding the Head, from which all the body by joints and bands having nourishment ministered, and knit together, increaseth with the increase of God. Wherefore if ye be dead with Christ from the rudiments of the world, why, as though living in the world, are ye subject to ordinances, (touch not; taste not; handle not; which all are to perish with the using;) after the commandments and doctrines of men? Which things have indeed a shew of wisdom in will worship,

and humility, and neglecting of the body: not in any honour to the satisfying of the flesh." **(Colossians 2:11-23)**

"*If ye then be risen with Christ, seek those things which are above, where Christ sitteth on the right hand of God.*" (Colossians 3:1)

B efore Adam and Eve were ever on this earth, a huge battle took place in Heaven. It began when someone said, "I will be like God."

There were three archangels of God. There is Michael, who often speaks about judgment in the Bible; Gabriel, who brings good news or "*tidings of great joy*"; and Lucifer, who was the most beautiful of the three. Lucifer was the one who felt he should be exalted above all others. This is detailed in Isaiah 14:12-14.

"*How art thou fallen from heaven, O Lucifer, son of the morning! how art thou cut down to the ground, which didst weaken the nations! For thou hast said in thine heart, I will ascend into heaven, I will exalt my throne above the stars of God: I will sit also upon the mount of the congregation, in the sides of the north: I will ascend above the heights of the clouds; I will be like the most High.*"

Five times in that passage Lucifer said, "I will be like God." But God will share His glory with no one, so Lucifer was "*brought down to hell, to the sides of the pit*" as we see in Isaiah 14:15.

Today Satan is doing everything he can to bring you away from where God wants you to be. He is the author of division in the guise of unity, encouraging all of us to do whatever we want and believe whatever we want.

Inside every one of us is an emptiness that only God can fill. In the time that Paul wrote this epistle to the Colossians, there was a degree of mysticism in that city, and many people felt that through mysticism they could find God. Astrology was evident in that era as it is today, with millions of people reading their daily horoscopes believing that they will find faith in them. Philosophy and legalism abounded among the Colossians, and these practices are prevalent.

Our challenge is to live our lives for Jesus Christ, knowing that only He can meet the deep-seated needs we have inside all of us.

Religion is a man-made proposition, while Christianity is about a relationship and a walk with Jesus Christ.

In his book *What's So Amazing About Grace?* Philip Yancey tells a story about a huge rock music concert many years ago in London's Wembley Stadium. Many of the people in the audience were under the influence of alcohol and drugs, and as the concert was coming to a close a lady took the stage to sing the final song of the night, an acappella version of "Amazing Grace."

As she finished the first verse and moved into the second, a hush fell over the massive crowd. By the time she was into the final verse, many were singing along with her. In an article in the next day's newspaper the writer wondered how something like that could have happened. The journalist concluded his thought by saying, "Everyone needs to have grace in their lives."

As we think about the freedom that we have in Christ, let's first consider the covenant relationship we have with Him that is outlined in verse 11: "*In whom also ye are circumcised with the circumcision made without hands, in putting off the body of the sins of the flesh by the circumcision of Christ.*"

God deals with His people using covenants and agreements. In this verse He tells us that we have a bond with Him not based upon circumcision. The Gnostics in Paul's day tried to convince people that Christ had not come in the flesh, and they stressed that some people were more spiritual than others based upon the issue of circumcision. They even said that paying attention to certain aspects of one's diet would make a person part of the spiritually elite.

But Paul already reminded the Colassians in the previous chapter what we have in Christ. In Colossians 1:18 he wrote, "*And he is the head of the body, the church: who is the beginning, the firstborn from the dead; that in all things he might have the preeminence.*" He provides everything we need to have a relationship with Him.

Circumcision was a physical ritual in the Old Testament that carried with it a deep spiritual significance. Spiritual circumcision is a circumcision of the heart, and in the New Testament we see a new kind of covenant relationship based solely upon what Christ has done for us.

In verses 12-13 he talks about baptism and the abundant life. *"Buried with him in baptism, wherein also ye are risen with him through the faith of the operation of God, who hath raised him from the dead. And you, being dead in your sins and the uncircumcision of your flesh, hath he quickened together with him, having forgiven you all trespasses."*

Why should a person be baptized? Some will say it is because Jesus was baptized or because others we can read about in the Bible were baptized. Those events, while they are true, are not the reason for us to do the same thing.

Baptism is an important event in a Christian's life. It is a command that we are to follow after we have accepted Christ, but it is also a statement that we are making. When we are baptized, we are saying, "I want to be identified with Jesus Christ. I am saying goodbye to the old life and hello to the new life." Baptism is the public identification of what Jesus Christ has done in your heart and that you will now be a follower of Him, ready to live the abundant life that He wants all of us to live.

Verse 14 is powerful. *"Blotting out the handwriting of ordinances that was against us, which was contrary to us, and took it out of the way, nailing it to his cross."* That word *"ordinances"* can also be translated as *"requirements."* This shows a stark contrast between what the law can do and what Christ can do for us.

As previously stated in chapter three, in the Old Testament we have the Ten Commandments, which is part of the foundation for the laws of any civilized society. However, they are not only meant to be placed on the wall of a government building or even a Christian building. They are God's requirements for righteousness in your life as well as mine.

The first commandment, listed in Exodus 20, states plainly that we are to worship only one God. None of us can say truthfully that we have worshipped only God every day of our lives. A spouse, a child, or a material possession has probably been in the way at some point. The same goes for the second commandment, as we all have had idols at various times that took the place of God.

Of course, you can go down the entire list and find that you have in some way violated every one of the commandments. It is not a comfortable feeling when you realize that you have fallen short so often regarding these requirements God has handed down to us. When we judge ourselves solely by the law, there is something very wrong with us.

If a judge sets a guilty man free, the law has been cheapened and the injured party is without restitution. How can we deal with this? As verse 14 shows us, those requirements were taken care of because on our own, we could never keep the law.

When Jesus died on the cross, He not only dealt with our sins but also with the law. In our case, the injured party is God the Father, who cannot allow sin into His presence. But at the cross it was as if a huge eraser was applied to our lives so that when God looks at us, He does so through the lens of the Lord Jesus Christ. The slate is absolutely clean – not because you kept the requirements of the law, but because He fulfilled the requirements.

This victory is emphasized in verse 15: "*And having spoiled principalities and powers, he made a shew of them openly, triumphing over them in it.*" In Roman times a general would lead the army to victory over opposing forces and return with the spoils, such as captives and territory. He would be given a parade known as the Parade of the Triumph. Likewise we know that in the battle of good and evil, Jesus Christ is the One who ultimately triumphs.

With all of this in mind, we should consider four reminders.

A spiritual experience with God leads to submission and service. Verse 16 says, "*Let no man therefore judge you in meat, or in drink, or in respect of a holy day, or of the new moon, or of the sabbath days.*" In Paul's day there were laws concerning diet or the observance of certain days. He is writing here to tell the Colossians that those do not necessarily lead to a relationship with God.

I Timothy 1:8 says, "*But we know that the law is good, if a man use it lawfully.*" That means using the law properly. Colossians 2:17 illustrates the importance of the law: "*Which are a shadow of things to come; but the body is of Christ.*"

Look at verse 18. "*Let no man beguile you of your reward in a voluntary humility and worshipping of angels, intruding into those things which he hath not seen, vainly puffed up by his fleshly mind.*" That verse talks about being cheated out of a reward. Once you come to Christ, you no longer have to worry about standing before God to be judged for your sins. You will one day give an account for how you lived your life for Christ, but nothing with regard to works will get us right with God. It is all about Christ.

A spiritual experience is not about rules and regulations. Historically there have been individuals who purposely slept on hard beds, beat themselves, would not talk for days, and adhered to strict dietary rules conjectured that this would somehow make them right with God.

A diet is good for your health. Observing certain days and traditions are not wrong. But if those disciplines are being applied for salvation, they have no use or merit whatsoever. This is made clear in verses 20-22.

"Wherefore if ye be dead with Christ from the rudiments of the world, why, as though living in the world, are ye subject to ordinances, (touch not; taste not; handle not; which all are to perish with the using;) after the commandments and doctrines of men?"

Why would one come back to these regulations? These are man-made regulations. That is the point of these verses for those who are in Christ. Verse 23 emphasizes the futility of following this path. *"Which things have indeed a shew of wisdom in will worship, and humility, and neglecting of the body: not in any honour to the satisfying of the flesh."* All of this means nothing when it comes to having a relationship with God.

My wife and I went out to eat recently with some friends, and I noticed on the menu that this particular restaurant offered liver and onions. I do not get this delicacy at home because my wife does not care to smell or taste liver, but since a recent surgery, I have felt the need to eat better and I think liver and onions make a healthy choice. I had that along with vegetables, and no one at the table had any interest in what was on my plate.

The waitress came back around asking about dessert. I refused. The couple dining with us were interested in dessert. She brought a platter of desserts and there was a huge piece of carrot cake. I changed my mind quickly.

"What about your desire to eat right?" my wife asked.

"I believe eating carrot cake **is** eating right."

I can try to stay physically fit (although that meal was not a huge success) and do all of the right things for my body and mind, but it means nothing when it comes to salvation. That is what the book of Colossians is teaching us – it is Jesus and Him alone.

Have you ever wondered why people seem to get so upset with Jesus? They don't act that way toward Mohammad or Buddha. Remember our earlier discussion about Lucifer's stated desire to be just like God, and that God cast him out of the heavenlies? Ever since then, Lucifer has done everything he can possibly do to detract from what Jesus Christ has done and to prevent us from having a victorious Christian life.

Satan has already been defeated. That happened when Jesus died, was buried and rose again. Satan is the loser, and Jesus Christ is the victor. With that in mind, our challenge today should be to focus on the freedom that we have in Him.

Chapter Seven

FOCUS ON TRANSFORMATION

"If ye then be risen with Christ, seek those things which are above, where Christ sitteth on the right hand of God. Set your affection on things above, not on things on the earth. For ye are dead, and your life is hid with Christ in God. When Christ, who is our life, shall appear, then shall ye also appear with him in glory. Mortify therefore your members which are upon the earth; fornication, uncleanness, inordinate affection, evil concupiscence, and covetousness, which is idolatry: For which things' sake the wrath of God cometh on the children of disobedience: In the which ye also walked some time, when ye lived in them. But now ye also put off all these; anger, wrath, malice, blasphemy, filthy communication out of your mouth. Lie not one to another, seeing that ye have put off the old man with his deeds; and have put on the new man, which is renewed in knowledge after the image of him that created him: Where there is neither Greek nor Jew, circumcision nor uncircumcision, Barbarian, Scythian, bond nor free: but Christ is all, and in all. Put on therefore, as the elect of God, holy and beloved, bowels of mercies, kindness, humbleness of mind, meekness, longsuffering; forbearing one another, and forgiving one another, if any man have a quarrel against any: Even as Christ forgave you, so also do ye. And above all these things put on charity, which is the bond of perfectness. And let the peace of God rule in your hearts, to the which also ye are called in one body; and be ye thankful. Let the word of

Christ dwell in you richly in all wisdom; teaching and admonishing one another in psalms and hymns and spiritual songs, singing with grace in your hearts to the Lord. And whatsoever ye do in word or deed, do all in the name of the Lord Jesus, giving thanks to God and the Father by him." **(Colossians 3:1-17)**

D oes the Christian life work? Can it work?
One day in the early years of our marriage, a man came to the door trying to sell my wife and me a vacuum sweeper. This was a popular method of selling at the time, and many people went door to door.

One of the first things the salesman did was emphasize how his product could clean up any amount of dirt and whatever mess we might make. We had a four-room house with about 800 square feet, and I really just wanted something to get the dirt off the floor.

The salesman had one problem. The entire time he was at our house, he could not get the machine to work. He tried unplugging and plugging it back in, asking if our fuses were out, and did everything he could think of, but it just wouldn't work. He left without selling us anything. It looked like a great machine, but it simply did not work.

Does the Christian life work? Warren Wiersbe said, "It does little good if Christians declare and defend the truth but fail to demonstrate it in their lives."

Back in Paul's day there were plenty of pagan religions that talked about issues and theology but said little or nothing about personal morality. Worshipping God is important, but when there is no change in one's lifestyle we have to wonder why.

II Corinthians 5:17 says, "*If any man be in Christ, he is a new creature.*" That means when Christ comes into your life there is a newness that takes over. These verses in the second chapter of Colossians look at the evidence of a changed life.

Verses 1-4 show us that one proof of this is our relationship with Christ Himself. Look at verse 1. "*If ye then be risen with Christ, seek those things which are above, where Christ sitteth on the right hand of God.*" The word "*if*" is the start of a rhetorical statement; some translations have the first word of that verse not "*if*" but "*since*," and that is probably a better translation. When Jesus Christ rose from the grave, you and I rose symbolically with Him. Our position is not a hypothetical situation or a lofty goal but a done deal.

Verses 2-3 tell us, *"Set your affection on things above, not on things on the earth. For ye are dead, and your life is hid with Christ in God."* Romans 6-8 remind us of the death of Christ and what it means, and that is reiterated here in verse 3. Christ died for us (substitution; He bears our penalty) and also with us (identification; breaking the power and spell of sin). You can get over whatever sin is holding you back in your life by setting your mind on the things of God and not this earth.

The latter portion of verse 3 suggests a unique position in our relationship with God. The Greek scholar A.T. Robertson put it this way: "So here we are in Christ, who is in God, and no burglar, not even Satan himself, can separate us from the love of God that is in Christ." No one can take away from you what God has given you through your faith in Jesus Christ. God loves you with an unconditional love that is given without apology, and because of this our motives must be heavenly.

Now look at verse 4. *"When Christ, who is our life, shall appear, then shall ye also appear with him in glory."* What a promise. Eternal life is ours in Christ, and that should give us zeal to live for the Lord.

I read a story about two sisters who lived a wild and wicked life before coming to Christ. They were given an invitation to a rowdy party and they sent this reply: "We regret that we cannot attend because we have died." That is the attitude we should have, because when you come to Christ there is a death (separation) that takes place as you leave your old life to begin living as a believer.

These verses we have read so far paint a very positive picture of our life in Christ. Now we must look at some of the specifics regarding how we should live, and these are no less important.

Verse 5 says, *"Mortify therefore your members which are upon the earth; fornication, uncleanness, inordinate affection, evil concupiscence, and covetousness, which is idolatry."* That word *"mortify"* means we are to put to death some things in our lives. Walking in Christ is all well and good, but there are also some things we need to be walking away from, and this verse lists some of them.

The first item is fornication, which means any kind of sexual immorality. God's plan for sex is meant for a man and a woman in marriage. Uncleanness is also mentioned, and that refers to lustful impurity connected to luxury and loose living. Inordinate affection occurs when the mind excites sexual impurity. Whenever you feed your mind certain things, those thoughts will come back to you in a flood and lead you to perform those things in your flesh, which is why one should stay away from pornography and other things that take us away from a holy life with God.

Evil desires are mentioned next along with covetousness, which is the sin of always wanting more and never being satisfied. Covetousness is compared to idolatry, which is as serious as anything mentioned in the Bible when the subject of sin is discussed. In all of the New Testament epistles there are lists of sins like this that God will deal with.

We began this chapter talking about the abundant life in Christ, which makes everyone feel good, but we must remember that there are things to be avoided if we are to remain in that abundant life.

Notice in verse 8: "*But now ye also put off all these; anger, wrath, malice, blasphemy, filthy communication out of your mouth.*" If you are wearing a jacket, think about it right now as a picture of sin in your life, the obvious response would be to take it off. Notice how he uses the word "*all*" here, as every sinful act mentioned is important.

The first three things listed in verse 8 – anger, wrath and malice – all come from the same root word. Wrath is a sudden outburst that stems from anger, and malice is an attitude of ill will toward another person. Sometimes we see someone else's success and become jealous, or we notice someone's trouble and get happy. Blasphemy is speech that is slanderous with the goal to down others. "*Filthy communication*" includes gossip and coarse or obscene language.

God wants us to put off these sins. This is not the idea of reforming oneself, but of completely eliminating these things from one's life.

Sometimes our upbringing as children or our circumstances relating to other people make it more difficult to simply "*put off*" these things that are toxic in our lives, but as we seek to walk properly with God we can take care of them as we should.

Verse 9 is very interesting. "*Lie not one to another, seeing that ye have put off the old man with his deeds.*" Satan is the liar, and when we lie, we are cooperating with Satan. His desire is for us to be deceived, and God does not want us to live like that.

Our sinful nature causes us to enter these sins. However, we need to seek what is above, as the opening verses of Colossians 3 talk about, but when we get into the specifics of verses 8-9 it can be difficult to deal with.

Verse 10 begins the discussion of our relationship to fellowship. "*And have put on the new man, which is renewed in knowledge after the image of him that created him.*" There are two Greek words that refer to the idea of something that is new. One of them speaks about the quality of something, and the other talks about being renewed.

So how do we become new? It is about knowledge. Our relationship is based upon our knowledge of God.

We were made in the very image of God – intellectually, emotionally, and every other way you can think of. Adam and Eve sinned in the beginning and that image was marred because of sin.

The Bible says that through Christ we become transformed into the very image and likeness of God. That is a truth that sets us free. It does not matter what your economic status might be, where you came from culturally or what position you hold. When we come to Christ, we all come on the same level – at the foot of the cross. Our relationship with Jesus Christ is not just about putting off things, but also putting on the knowledge of Him.

Verse 11 says, "*Where there is neither Greek nor Jew, circumcision nor uncircumcision, Barbarian, Scythian, bond nor free: but Christ is all, and in all.*" In Christ there are no nationalities or cultural differences, and there is no economic or political status. The Greeks considered all non-Greeks to be barbarians, which is why the reference in verse 11 is necessary. It doesn't matter what your past has been; Christ has everything you need and through Him you can be brought back into the fellowship of God.

Look at verse 12 and our relationship to motivation. "*Put on therefore, as the elect of God, holy and beloved, bowels of mercies, kindness, humbleness of mind, meekness, longsuffering.*"

In that verse we see a reference to God's elect. To better understand this truth, we need to look in the Old Testament and see in Deuteronomy 7:7-8 why God chose the nation of Israel. "*The LORD did not set his love upon you, nor choose you, because ye were more in number than any people; for ye were the fewest of all people: But because the LORD loved you, and because he would keep the oath which he had sworn unto your fathers, hath the LORD brought you out with a mighty hand, and redeemed you out of the house of bondmen, from the hand of Pharaoh king of Egypt.*"

God took the children of Israel out of Egypt because it was what He wanted to do. God loves you because He has chosen to love you. We do not deserve to be loved, but God loves us because that is His choice. What a wonderful thought.

We see in Colossians 3:12 the phrase "*bowels of mercies.*" This means exactly what it says. You might tell someone, "I love you with all my heart." In Paul's day someone may tell you that he loves you with all of his intestines. I don't recommend doing that today, but that was the thought at that time. It suggested an emotional response without reservation.

In the Old Testament there is a story about David's desire to be a blessing to his dear friend Jonathan's family (II Samuel 9). He inquired about the existence of any living members of Jonathan's household, and a servant in the king's house told him of a young crippled man named Mephibosheth, Jonathan's son.

The ninth chapter of II Samuel tells us how Mephibosheth bowed before King David thinking that perhaps something bad might happen to him. Imagine what he thought when David told him that he would be living in the palace and eating at the king's table the rest of his life. Mephibosheth asked why he would receive such special treatment, and he learned that it was because of his relationship to Jonathan.

Just as he received kindness because he was Jonathan's son, we are the recipients of God's kindness due to our relationship with

Christ. We should always be mindful of this as we live out our lives for Him.

Verse 12 also mentions humility, which is not something that was looked upon favorably during this time. The word translated as *"meekness"* is a soothing word almost like a healing medicine, and the three attributes of meekness, longsuffering and forbearance are used here in tandem because they work together. The thought is continued in verse 13: *"Forbearing one another, and forgiving one another, if any man have a quarrel against any: even as Christ forgave you, so also do ye."*

This is done with love and peace, as we see in verses 14-15. *"And above all these things put on charity, which is the bond of perfectness. And let the peace of God rule in your hearts, to the which also ye are called in one body; and be ye thankful."*

The word *"rule"* in verse 15 is an athletic term that suggests a game and the idea of prizes at the end of the game. From there we see the connection to thankfulness or praise. Peace brings praise and praise brings us back to peace.

Look at verse 16. *"Let the word of Christ dwell in you richly in all wisdom; teaching and admonishing one another in psalms and hymns and spiritual songs, singing with grace in your hearts to the Lord."* There were many false teachers in Paul's day who tried to harmonize the Word of God with their own teaching. The word *"dwell"* in this verse means His Word will feel at home in your mind and your heart. The poverty of Scripture is everywhere today, but when you have the Word in your life there is a song in your heart, as evidenced by the final words of verse 16.

I was walking down the hallway of Dade Christian School in Miami, Florida one day after hours, when very few people were around. Suddenly I heard a few people singing a song at the top of their lungs. When I came around the corner and met them, there was a hint of embarrassment.

"Don't be embarrassed," I said. "Let's sing it together."

We did just that. Of course, they sounded much better than I did, but we sang as one. When you have Christ in your life, there is indeed a song in your heart.

You and I cannot allow circumstances to dictate how we react in our lives. The Word of God should be the only thing that dictates our actions.

Verse 17 once again emphasizes where our priorities need to be. *"And whatsoever ye do in word or deed, do all in the name of the Lord Jesus, giving thanks to God and the Father by him."*

In ancient times, names were very important. In the Bible three times we have the word Christian (Acts 11:26, Acts 26:28, I Peter 4:16). That term was often viewed with contempt during New Testament times, but this verse stresses the idea that all we do should be in the name of Christ, as He is all that we will ever need.

Often someone can name their denomination – Episcopalian, Catholic, Lutheran, Baptist, Wesleyan, Methodist, or whatever – and no one will get upset or even care about it. However, when one makes it known they are a follower of Jesus Christ, people quickly form opinions. Let me challenge you today to never be ashamed of being a child of God.

Throughout the book of Colossians we read verses about thanks-giving or being thankful to God (Colossians 1:3, 1:12, 2:7, 3:15, 3:17, 4:2) for who He is and what He has done in our lives. In Colossians 3 we read about forgiveness (v. 13), peace (v. 15), having the Word in us (v. 16), and all of the ways we identify with Christ.

If you find a new automobile, and it is exactly what you always wanted to have – it feels right, it looks right, it smells right – but you turn the key and the engine doesn't start, would you buy it?

If you train to be an airplane pilot, and you taxi a plane up and down the runway but never get it up in the air, what kind of pilot would you be?

As a child of God, you are not just here to wander aimlessly through life and get to Heaven someday. You are here for more than just "Sunday Christianity." If our faith is real, we will put off and put on the appropriate things and we will do so willingly because Jesus has done something in our hearts to change us through the power of the Gospel. You will get up on Monday morning and live out the faith during the week, not just at church on Sunday. God will then open doors of opportunities.

I came home one afternoon during a busy day and found a man walking around my house. He was the meter reader. He was new on the job and couldn't find my meter, so I showed him where it was. When I walked in the house, he came in right behind me. That made me nervous.

"How are you doing?" I asked.

He shook his head. "I'm not really doing well at all."

I had actually come back home to pick up some things I had forgotten, so I was in a hurry and didn't have time to hear about his problems. I asked him anyway.

"What's the problem?"

He began to tell me about his home and his family. I'm not sure why he even told me these things. As I walked into my kitchen to pick up a few items, he kept talking. Finally, I asked him, "Sir, if you died today, do you know for sure that you would go to Heaven?"

"No, I don't know that."

"Would you like to know?"

"Yes," he replied. "I need something."

I shared with him the wonderful story of the Gospel, about how we are all sinners and how Jesus died, was buried and rose again. I told him that Jesus was the one and only Savior, and we knelt down together in my kitchen as he bowed his head asked Christ to save him.

I was busy and had a lot on my mind that day. Today, however, I could not tell you what I was so concerned about. I don't even remember what I forgot that day that required my return home. I do know that God in His sovereignty allowed it because someone needed Him.

We all need to seek those things that are above and be concerned far more about spiritual things than earthly things. God is transforming His people. Center your mind on Him and His Word and enjoy the transformation.

Chapter Eight

FOCUS ON RELATIONSHIP

"Wives, submit yourselves unto your own husbands, as it is fit in the Lord. Husbands, love your wives, and be not bitter against them. Children, obey your parents in all things: for this is well pleasing unto the Lord. Fathers, provoke not your children to anger, lest they be discouraged. Servants, obey in all things your masters according to the flesh; not with eyeservice, as menpleasers; but in singleness of heart, fearing God; and whatsoever ye do, do it heartily, as to the Lord, and not unto men; knowing that of the Lord ye shall receive the reward of the inheritance: for ye serve the Lord Christ. But he that doeth wrong shall receive for the wrong which he hath done: and there is no respect of persons. Masters, give unto your servants that which is just and equal; knowing that ye also have a Master in heaven." **(Colossians 3:18 – 4:1)**

To understand the emphasis on relationships we must grasp that the previous section of Colossians refers to the Word of Christ dwelling in us. Our lives need to reflect the Lord in a Christ-like way. The parallel passage to this section is Ephesians 5:18 – 6:4. In the Ephesians passage we are told to be filled with the Spirit of God. In our study of Colossians we are told to be filled with the Word of God. It is only as the Holy Spirit and the Word of God fill us that we are to live Christ-like as wives, husbands, parents, children, masters, and servants.

The word for submit in the passage is a military term. It means to "rank under". John Philips in his commentary on Colossians quotes scholar Handley Moule who prefers the rendering "be loyal". It is perhaps the best idea of submission in the husband-wife context. The wife needs to understand, acknowledge, and give to her husband his God ordained position of leadership. She is not to be considered second class, inferior or a slave. The teaching is one of order in the home. The instructions are addressed to the "how" of a home. Husbands are to love their wives. The Greek word for love is agape. This is the strongest form of love and it describes our Savior's love given at the cross. In verse nineteen, husbands are warned not to be bitter. The word means to irritate or exasperate.

Bitterness must not sorrow our marriages. Husbands need to cultivate a sweet, loving, tender spirit. The wife then is to submit (vv. 18) as it is "fit in the Lord". The word means to arrive at a goal.

The passage leaves the husband and wife relationship and goes toward the family. God's moral government begins in the home. Parents are to set the standards and rules for the family. A child is to obey their parents in all things. This learning prepares the way for the child to accept larger roles of authority. If a child does not learn obedience at home, they will grow to disrespect all authority – school, police, employment, and ultimately they will struggle with God's authority. This is a very important principle to teach our children. God views disobedience the same as witchcraft (I Samuel 15:22-23). Children please the Lord as they obey their parents.

A word is then given to fathers. "Do not provoke your children." The word provoke means to "rouse to anger, or incite, or irritate." The father's role is to be a dad who leads, not a dictator who causes irritation. To do this will discourage the children. The word for discouraged means to dishearten the children. Breaking the will prevents defiance but breaking the spirit promotes discouragement. A parent should set standards, limits, and enforce discipline. To accomplish this there must be the filling of the Word of God (and Spirit Ephesians 5:18). Two excellent Old Testament works that provide insight on these issues are Ecclesiastes and Proverbs. Read them slowly noting the family relationships. Apply them then, to your lives.

The next relationship deals with servants. The employee/ employer relationship is addressed in the servant/master relationship. A servant is one under the authority of another. The principle of the scriptures is the same. The word for 'obey' in verse 22 is the same word used in verse 20 when it refers to children and allegiance to parents. This is a principle of obeying duly delegated authority. The word translated as eyeservice in the Greek text is (ὀςθαλμοδουλεία) ophthalmodoulia and it has the sense of doing what the boss says only when the leader is watching. Then when the employer is not looking to ignore them! This is disrespectful, a bad attitude, and is ultimately playing the part of a hypocrite. The Christian position is singleness of heart. We are to serve our employers with the fear of God. The testimony we have for Jesus Christ is often observed at the work place.

The concluding thoughts deal with our day to day activities. They are to be done heartily which means "from the heart". What we do is to the Lord. Verses 23 and 24 remind us that we can receive the inheritance of the Lord which reminds us that we will one day appear at the Judgment seat of Christ and give an account of our lives (II Corinthians 5:10). This is not for salvation purposes but for rewarding purposes. "For you serve the Lord Christ" is in the present tense which means that whatever we are doing is to be done unto the Lord.

A reminder is then presented of unrighteousness. A warning is given to Christians: Do not lose your reward! A proper day to day relationship for masters in their relationship to servants begins chapter 4 but is obviously connected closely to chapter 3. The word equal refers to fair. In matters of compensation, a master must be fair. What a contrast this is in compensation to the enormous greed that is in the hearts of so many Americans!

Chapter Nine

FOCUS ON FAITHFULNESS

"Continue in prayer, and watch in the same with thanksgiving; withal praying also for us, that God would open unto us a door of utterance, to speak the mystery of Christ, for which I am also in bonds: That I may make it manifest, as I ought to speak. Walk in wisdom toward them that are without, redeeming the time. Let your speech be always with grace, seasoned with salt, that ye may know how ye ought to answer every man. All my state shall Tychicus declare unto you, who is a beloved brother, and a faithful minister and fellowservant in the Lord: Whom I have sent unto you for the same purpose, that he might know your estate, and comfort your hearts; with Onesimus, a faithful and beloved brother, who is one of you. They shall make known unto you all things which are done here. Aristarchus my fellow prisoner saluteth you, and Marcus, sister's son to Barnabas, (touching whom ye received commandments: if he come unto you, receive him;) and Jesus, which is called Justus, who are of the circumcision. These only are my fellowworkers unto the kingdom of God, which have been a comfort unto me. Epaphras, who is one of you, a servant of Christ, saluteth you, always labouring fervently for you in prayers, that ye may stand perfect and complete in all the will of God. For I bear him record, that he hath a great zeal for you, and them that are in Laodicea, and them in Hierapolis. Luke, the beloved physician, and Demas, greet you. Salute the brethren which are in Laodicea, and Nymphas, and the church which is in

his house. And when this epistle is read among you, cause that it be read also in the church of the Laodiceans; and that ye likewise read the epistle from Laodicea. And say to Archippus, take heed to the ministry which thou hast received in the Lord, that thou fulfill it. The salutation by the hand of me Paul. Remember my bonds. Grace be with you. Amen." **(Colossians 4:2-18)**

It is a huge blessing when you have someone in your life who is trusted and faithful. In this passage Paul writes about some people who were very close to him and how they lived out their lives.

I read an interesting story about Will Houghton, who was pastor at Calvary Baptist Church in New York City and also at the Baptist Tabernacle in Atlanta. At one of his pastorates a man in the church investigated him to see about his background. His conclusion was this: "His life matches his preaching."

What a great challenge. None of us want to see someone snooping around in our lives, but we should all stop to consider if we are living in a way that matches what we say. In the fourth chapter of Colossians we see a number of men in Paul's life who were faithful to what God had called them to do.

Notice in verses 2-4 that the discipline of faithfulness is seen, first of all, in the matter of prayer. *"Continue in prayer, and watch in the same with thanksgiving; Withal praying also for us, that God would open unto us a door of utterance, to speak the mystery of Christ, for which I am also in bonds: That I may make it manifest, as I ought to speak."*

Paul wrote this epistle from jail. He was there because he had been preaching the Word of God and reaching the Gentiles. Nowhere in the book of Colossians do we see Paul praying to escape from jail. Instead, Paul prayed that he might remain faithful to his calling and continue to reach the Gentiles with the Gospel.

The Bible says in I Thessalonians 5:17, *"Pray without ceasing."* That is what Paul was doing here. As you notice in verse 3, he did not pray for his release from prison, but that he would have the opportunity to proclaim the Word of God in whatever forum the Lord wanted him to do so.

When you pray, do you pray in generalities or in specifics? Do you ask God to "bless all the missionaries" or do you call them by name? Do you ask Him to "bless my family" or do you talk to Him about your family members as individuals and cite their respective needs?

One day when our two-year-old granddaughter was at our house we sat down for a meal and asked her if she would like to pray. At this particular time I was hungry and hoped she would say something short. Instead, she prayed for me several times and also for her grandma, her sister, and even the toys in her room. I said "amen" a few times and she kept right on praying. She was praying for specific things.

Prayer, to be effective, needs to be specific. It is not something we do lightly. Prayer is not intended to get man's will done in Heaven, but to get God's will done on Earth.

Look at I John 5:14-15. "*And this is the confidence that we have in him, that, if we ask any thing according to his will, he heareth us: And if we know that he hear us, whatsoever we ask, we know that we have the petitions that we desired of him.*" Notice the words "*according to his will.*"

Several years ago I preached at Liberty University in Lynchburg, Va. I was invited by the vice-president, Sumner Wemp, to supper. He told me, "Be ready tonight at eight o'clock. I'm going to pick you up and take you out for one of the best steak dinners in town."

We went to a steak house and the dinner was tremendous; I liked it so much that I did not think I listened to very much of what he said that night. However, he asked me a very interesting question.

"Do you often have daily answers to your prayers?" he asked.

Instead of answering him directly, I responded by asking him about his own experiences. He told me that he had been snowed in at a recent conference and spent considerable time studying various passages in the Bible about prayer.

"I believe that there are some prayer requests that God will answer that very day, if you will just pray for them," Wemp told me.

He said that he never had a new car in his life until he began to pray for one. In a short time a brand-new car was given to him, and it was completely paid for. When he said that, he had my full attention.

Then he reminded me of Psalm 37:4. "*Delight thyself also in the LORD: and he shall give thee the desires of thine heart.*" That is the key. When we pray, it is so that God can place us properly to guide us in life.

Richard Baxter wrote: "Prayer is not overcoming God's reluctance, but laying hold of God's willingness."

Back in Colossians 1:9-12, Paul wrote about his prayer for the people at Colosse. He was praying for them to be filled with the will of God and the Word of God. Often we do not pray about being the kind of person God wants us to be.

After the emphasis on prayer in the first part of Colossians 4, Paul addresses the topic of witnessing. Look at verses 5-6. "*Walk in wisdom toward them that are without, redeeming the time. Let your speech be always with grace, seasoned with salt, that ye may know how ye ought to answer every man.*"

In the first part of verse 5, "*them that are without*" are those who are not in the family of God, and the admonition to "*walk in wisdom*" is meant for us to always be conscious of our daily conduct and not do anything that would make it difficult for us to share the gospel.

If you have a bad reputation at work or you live a life that is inconsistent with Christian values, how can you share the gospel? We need to be careful how we live because there are always enemies of the gospel who oppose its spreading. Paul had many such enemies, but he lived a life that was consistent with what he preached and wrote.

Our country has tremendous problems today – moral problems, economic challenges, and even trouble amongst the people of God. We need revival today in the United States of America, starting in the churches. God needs to do a great work, and it begins in your heart when you become honest and transparent, realizing that there is a lost and dying world in need of Jesus Christ.

After addressing the discipline of faithfulness, Paul begins to talk about the diligence of faithfulness and names certain people in his life. Take a look at this list, starting with verses 7-8.

"*All my state shall Tychicus declare unto you, who is a beloved brother, and a faithful minister and fellowservant in the Lord: Whom*

I have sent unto you for the same purpose, that he might know your estate, and comfort your hearts."

The word *"beloved"* in verse 7 means "much love." *"Faithful servant"* means that he is a loyal servant, and *"fellowservant in the Lord"* shows that he worked alongside Paul and was appreciated.

Paul needed someone to tell others about his faith and what it was like to be in jail. There was no e-mail, newspaper or telephone in those days; messages were passed along by people as they traveled. The man chosen to perform this important task for Paul was Tychicus, who went to others and said, "I want to tell you about the ministry of the Apostle Paul." He was cited by Paul in the closing verses of Ephesians in the same way.

Verse 9 says, *"With Onesimus, a faithful and beloved brother, who is one of you. They shall make known unto you all things which are done here."* We see the phrase *"one of you"* that suggests Onesimus is known already to the Colossians, and he is given a job similar to Tychicus in that he will update the church on what is happening with Paul.

It is likely that the sun never sets on the ministry of a mission-minded church. Many missionaries are going through persecution and heartache, and around the world today there are more martyrs for the cause of Christ than at any time in the history of the church. When we hear reports like this from the mission field, as the churches did in Paul's day, we must continue to pray for them and never forget that they are servants of the most high God.

One of the great characteristics a person can be known for is faithfulness. These friends of Paul in the fourth chapter of Colossians were examples of this.

Look at verse 10. *"Aristarchus my fellow prisoner saluteth you, and Marcus, sister's son to Barnabas (touching whom ye received commandments: if he come unto you, receive him)."*

Here is a greeting from Aristarchus, who was in jail with Paul. Notice that it was not a complaint, but a friendly greeting. Aristarchus was originally from Thessalonica and stayed with Paul no matter the circumstances. Talk about a faithful friend. He was in prison with Paul.

Someone once said, "A friend walks in when everyone else walks out." If you have such a friend, you have a prized possession. We really don't know much about Aristarchus, but we know he was a faithful friend.

Marcus is actually Barnabas' cousin John Mark, who went AWOL during their first missionary journey. Paul became angry with John Mark and they were on the outs for a while, but that relationship had apparently been repaired here as Paul instructs the Colossians to welcome him.

Prior to his death, Paul gave Timothy this charge: "*Only Luke is with me. Take Mark, and bring him with thee: for he is profitable to me for the ministry.*"

I believe one of the unique truths of the Bible is that we have a God of another chance. If you feel that you have blown it as far as your life is concerned, do not think for a moment that God is finished with you. Don't worry about what other people say about you; make things right and you can count on God to be forgiving. Most of us would be in a lot of trouble if we did not have another chance. Paul had no use for John Mark at one time (perhaps Paul's own temper was part of the problem), but they reconciled and continued to be effective in the work of the Lord.

Verse 11 says, "*And Jesus, which is called Justus, who are of the circumcision. These only are my fellowworkers unto the kingdom of God, which have been a comfort unto me.*"

Jesus was actually a common name in this day. This man was a Jewish man, as we see from the phrase "*of the circumcision,*" and he was very helpful to Paul during his ministry.

We see in verses 12-13 another important coworker. "*Epaphras, who is one of you, a servant of Christ, saluteth you, always labouring fervently for you in prayers, that ye may stand perfect and complete in all the will of God. For I bear him record, that he hath a great zeal for you, and them that are in Laodicea, and them in Hierapolis.*"

Looking at these verses, along with Colossians 1:7-8, one could easily assume that Epaphras was the pastor of the church at Colosse. Paul had not met the Colossians when he wrote this epistle, and he pointed out in the first chapter that what he knew of them had been gleaned from Epaphras. We see here also that Epaphras was a prayer warrior – he prayed specifically, definitely and sacrificially. English cleric John Stott once said, "Prayer that costs nothing accomplishes nothing."

Verse 14 says, "*Luke, the beloved physician, and Demas, greet you.*" We know Luke as the doctor who wrote the book of Acts as well as the gospel that bears his own name.

Notice in particular the reference to Demas. In this verse Paul does not use any of the glowing adjectives that he does with the others. Demas was a man who was a respected fellow worker in the Lord at one time. But Paul writes later in II Timothy 4:10, "*For Demas hath forsaken me, having loved this present world, and is departed unto Thessalonica.*" These are sad words.

It is not easy to live as a Christian – actually, it is impossible – unless you are constantly in the Word of God and in prayer and letting the spirit guide you. Demas let the world get into his life until it overtook him.

You will have challenges in your life. There will be times that other Christians disappoint you, and at other times you will disappoint yourself. Circumstances will make it difficult for you and cause you to wonder how you can continue to serve the Lord. If you turn back toward the world, it will be even more difficult for you the rest of your life. However, serving Jesus is always worthwhile. Paul's references to Demas in these two passages can serve as a warning to us not to become like Demas but to remain faithful. We have decisions to make every day that can affect our walk with God, and we would be wise to keep this in mind as we go through the Christian life.

Verse 15 introduces us to Nymphas, who opened his house to the church so its members could meet there. Verse 16 mentions "*the epistle from Laodicea,*" which was not part of the inspired Word of God but one of many other letters Paul likely wrote during his ministry.

Verse 17 says, "*And say to Archippus, take heed to the ministry which thou hast received in the Lord, that thou fulfil it.*" That is an admonition which can serve as a reminder to all of us that God has a definite purpose for every one of His servants.

The book of Colossians closes in verse 18 with these words: *"The salutation by the hand of me Paul. Remember my bonds. Grace be with you. Amen."* Paul makes one final reference to the fact that he is in jail – not to complain or ask that he be released, but so that his fellow Christians will simply remember.

Martin Luther was the great reformer. There is a great deal that has been written about Luther, but very little about a man named Melancthon. Luther once called on Melancthon, whom he thought was dying, and said, "You can't die. I need you." Melancthon did much of the work, along with much prayer, and gave stability to Martin Luther when he needed it.

When you see a church or some other ministry and the people who lead it, there are always many others behind the scenes doing much of the work that must be done. Paul uses most of the fourth chapter of Colossians to let everyone know how thankful he was for them. They were faithful, and we should challenge ourselves to live our lives the same way.

There is a phrase in the book of Lamentations that was the basis for one of the most-loved hymns in the church: *"Great is thy faithfulness."* Our God is a faithful God. The people cited by Paul in the closing verses of Colossians understood this, and they also understood the cross – the death, burial and resurrection of Jesus Christ. That should motivate us to live our lives for Him.

We do not know when the end of our life will be, but when it comes, we should all hope others will say of us that we lived in a way that matched what we said.

Conclusion

The book of Colossians is written by the Apostle Paul from a dingy prison cell. The apostle's message is one of focus. This particular volume on Colossians "He must be the one" reminds us to focus on the trinity, prayer, Lordship, purpose, maturity, freedom, transformation, relationship, and faithfulness. Yet the major theme is the preeminent Christ. The Colossians epistle is to remind us of the excellence that there is in Jesus Christ. The encouragement for every faithful follower of our Lord is to learn of him and follow him. There is no one else who is worthy of such attention. He must be worshiped!

I opened this book with Tom Wallace's story about the sign he saw in an obscure service station that stated: "There's no place, like this place, anywhere near this place, so this must be the place." This reminds me of the symbolic thought – "There's no one Savior, like this Savior, anywhere near this Savior – He must be the one!" There is no one like Jesus.

Perhaps, my reader friend, you have never studied or focused on Jesus Christ. My encouragement to you is do more than study Him. My encouragement is to know Him. The scripture teaches us that we are all sinners. Romans 3:23 explains, "For all have sinned and come short of the Glory of God." Sin is to miss the mark. God is perfect and holy and sin is to miss the mark of God's perfection. We are all sinners. I am a sinner, you are, we all are. Doing better does not allow us to reach perfection with God. Titus 3:5 states, "Not by works or righteousness…"

Many good things like feeding the hungry, church membership, baptism, Bible studies, doing good deeds for the elderly, and a plethora of other things will not make us righteous before God. The problem is that our works do not satisfy a holy God! The net result is that death comes to all. Death is not the end. Death is a separation. Physical death is when the soul leaves the body. Spiritual death is when the soul is separated from God for eternity.

The sole purpose of Jesus Christ coming to the earth was to save sinners. "For the son of man is come to seek and to save those who are lost" (Luke 19:10). Jesus died to take away your sins. He was buried to bury your sins. He rose proving He is the Son of God. *"For I delivered to you first of all that which I also received: that Christ died for our sins according to the Scriptures, and that He was buried, and that He rose again the third day according to the Scriptures, and that He was seen by Cephas, then by the twelve"* (I Corinthians 15:3-5). When one realizes they are lost and need a Savior, there is but one thing to do. One must find a Savior! The Bible says in Romans 10:9 & 10:13 *"that if you confess with your mouth the Lord Jesus and believe in your heart that God has raised Him from the dead, you will be saved"*; *"For 'whoever calls on the name of the LORD shall be saved.'"* I cannot save you; I can help you with a prayer that can save you. Pray in your heart something like this: 'Lord I know I am a sinner, I cannot save myself. I recognize that Jesus is the only Savior. I here now ask him to take my sins and to forgive me and I trust him fully to be my Savior'. If you did that, drop me an email note: dpedrone@davisny.edu.

As you journey through your life, there is one thing you know for sure. "Jesus... He must be the one!

CPSIA information can be obtained at www.ICGtesting.com

259926BV00002B/1/P

9 781612 155166